A LESSON PLAN FOR

WOOD TURNING

Step-By-Step Instructions for
Mastering Woodturning Fundamentals

JAMES RODGERS

Linden Publishing
Fresno

A Lesson Plan for Woodturning
by James Rodgers

ISBN: 978-1-61035-181-2

135798642

Woodworking is inherently dangerous. Your safety is your
responsibility. Neither Linden Publishing nor the author
assume any responsibility for any injuries or accidents.

Printed in China

Library of Congress Cataloging-in-Publication Data

Rodgers, James, 1941 November 16-
    A lesson plan for woodturning : step-by-step instructions for mastering
woodturning fundamentals / James Rodgers.
        pages cm ISBN 978-1-61035-181-2 (pbk.)
    1. Turning (Lathe work)--Technique--Textbooks. 2. Woodwork--Patterns--
Textbooks. I. Title.
    TT201.R64 2014
    684'.083--dc23
                                        2013038215

Linden Publishing, Inc.
2006 S. Mary
Fresno, CA 93721
www.lindenpub.com

Contents

Preface vi

Preparing for Woodturning Activities viii

1. Getting Started—Turning Between Centers . . . 1

2. Keeping Your Tools Sharp 11

3. Your First Projects 20

4. Introduction to Faceplate Turning 35

5. Turning Your First Bowl 42

6. Turning Your First Platter 48

7. Working with Green Wood 54

8. Turning a Natural Edge Bowl 59

9. End Grain Turning 63

10. End Grain Boxes—Making Things Fit 67

11. Completing Your Projects 73

12. Where to Go Next 79

Appendix I: Additional Projects 80

Appendix II: Lathe Maintenance 90

Appendix III: Additional References 93

Preface

The goal of this volume is to provide a structured order to the teaching of woodturning skills utilizing safe and secure techniques. The information, instructions, and activities have been selected for this volume from several years' experience in teaching woodturning basics to both adult and younger students. Each activity is a chance to practice one technique on a usable project. Each following project builds by adding additional complexity to the earlier projects.

The opening text is what you need to know to proceed on to the following activity.

While there are many different techniques and approaches to teaching yourself or others woodturning, the approach presented in this book distills methods and processes used both in adult and high school classes for over a decade and are known to achieve the desired learning results.

Follow the chapters in sequence. Read or deliver the discussions first and you or your students will develop a solid foundation in woodturning.

How to Use This Book

If you are a teacher

Read, study and deliver the written materials in the sequence presented followed by the appropriate reinforcing project activity. At the end of each chapter, it would be helpful to reinforce what has been learned with a discussion of what worked well and what could be done differently if the activity was repeated.

Most activities can be completed in about a three-hour time period, recognizing that that time may be broken into many smaller units by the nature of class schedules.

The full course, not including the additional activities, can be complete in about 60 hours.

The lessons are arranged in an order that most efficiently develops the skills necessary to turn wood safely:

- Turning between centers builds basic turning skills and muscle memory.
- Bowl turning adds additional tools and working with cross grain wood.
- Goblets and boxes introduce the student to the additional techniques of working with end grain and more precise techniques.
- Additional activities have been placed in the appendix for use with rapidly progressing learners or for additional practice.

A Bill of Materials for all activities has been included in the appendix to allow for ordering of supplies.

Teaching yourself

If the lessons are followed in sequence the completion of the basic instruction will take you through activities which you can repeat as many times as desired.

At the end of each activity, a self-evaluation should compare your results with what was anticipated; self-criticism will lead to improvement of techniques, and repetition will lead to skill.

Acknowledgements

The author wishes to thank the following people for their cooperation in the development of the materials and the production of this book.

Dr. Rosalind Harper for her assistance in the photography of the majority of the book's illustrations.

Jan Blumer and Mike Bulat for their assistance in additional photography.

Ron Kersey for developing all the Sketch Up drawings used.

The Wood Turning Center at the Pleasant Hill Education Center of the Mt. Diablo Unified School District where we have conducted woodturning classes for many years.

Sharon Rodgers for her review and editing of this writer's poor grammar.

Preparing for Woodturning Activities

Discussion

Successful woodturning requires a safe and comfortable environment, as well as all the necessary tools and accessories. Before getting started, here are a few things you need to know and address.

Setup for comfort and ease

Lathe height should be adjusted to allow the student to work without strain to the shoulders and back. If the spindle height of the lathe falls at the student's elbow height they will work with less fatigue. If your lathes are of a fixed height, a movable platform may be useful for the shorter student.

Allow sufficient room around each work location so as not to crowd the student and allow space for the instructor to comfortably work with each student. Five feet clearance left, right and behind the work location is a good average clearance.

Woodturning Safety Guidelines

When turning wood there are several safety guidelines to be observed rigorously:

- Safety glasses with side shields are always a minimum requirement.
- Full-face shields are added for bowl turning, where more protection is needed.
- Dust mask for lung protection is needed, especially during sanding.
- Closed toe shoes for comfort and safety at all times.
- Hands and forearms must be free of clothing and loose jewelry.
- Long hair must be pulled back.

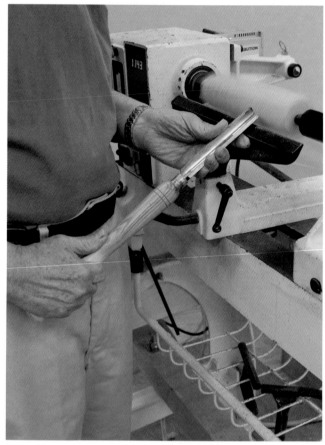

This is a good starting position and a comfortable stance.

- No ear buds for music or cell phones are allowed.

Additional safety rules with more general application are included in the appendix.

A LESSON PLAN FOR

WOOD
TURNING

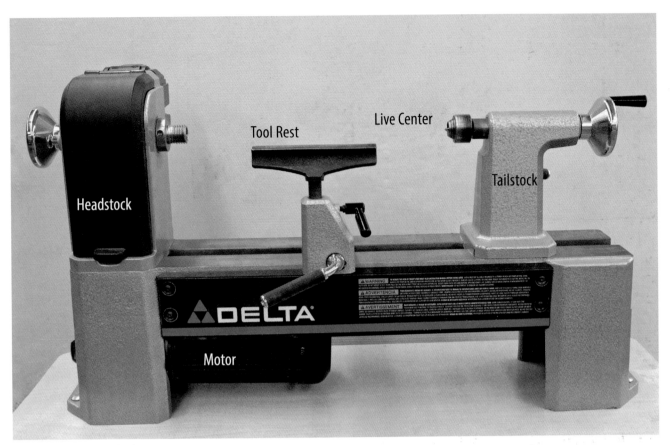

Here are the key lathe components.

Three aids to reducing accidents in a classroom setting
- Don't work when you are tired or unwell.
- Don't hurry or rush to complete a project.
- Recognize that there will always be distractions that can cause loss of focus.

Woodturning Terminology
There are a number of terms and names used to describe woodturning tools and activities. You'll find these terms introduced as needed throughout the book. Additional terminology is located in Appendix III.

Basic Tool List
Lathes should be equipped with a set of five basic turning tools. Other tools less frequently used can be held in a central location for shared use. Here is the basic set:
- Spindle roughing gouge. 1" diameter (approx.)
- Skew chisel, not round or oval stock. ¾"–1"
- Parting tool. ³⁄₁₆"–¼"
- Shallow-fluted gouge (spindle). ⅜"
- Deep fluted gouge (bowl). ¼"–⅜"

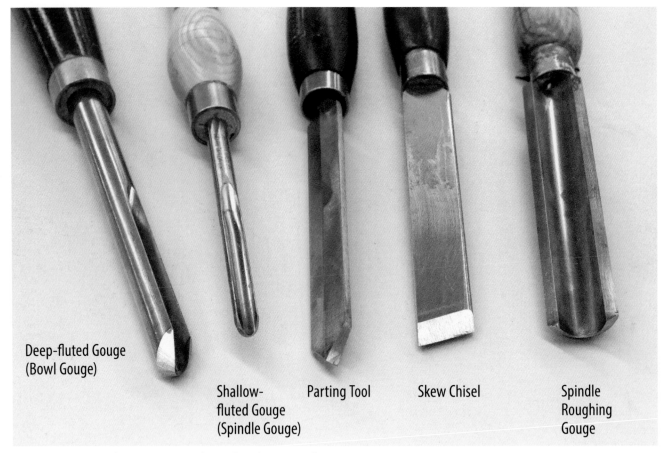

Deep-fluted Gouge
(Bowl Gouge)

Shallow-
fluted Gouge
(Spindle Gouge)

Parting Tool

Skew Chisel

Spindle
Roughing
Gouge

Your starting tool set contains these five basic tools.

Other accessories that each lathe will require

- Four-jaw scroll chuck with screw chuck accessory.
- ⅜" collet chuck with draw bar.
- Jacobs chuck with Morris taper #2 and selected drill bits.

Other tools to be shared might include

- 1" and 1½" interior bowl scrapers.
- ⅝"–1" inch round-nosed box scrapers.
- Calipers, wall thickness and vernier.

Things to Watch Out For

Here are the several things that always seem to cause beginners some difficulties:

- Tight body. This means a lack of freedom of movement, which restricts fluid motions, with the tools causing poor shaping of the project and irregular surfaces due to inadequate tool control. Rigid, tight muscles locking the tool tightly in the hand force the student to fight the wood/lathe combination, tires them, and can cause them to lose control.

- Working too fast. Forcing the tool through the wood, rather than understanding how fast the wood wants to be cut with that tool and at that lathe speed, creates rough surfaces and poorly shaped cuts. Cutting the wood before planning the best approach to the cut causes a lot of starting over. Think ahead. Don't start without an overall plan of what shape is to be achieved and how best to approach the final result. Many turners will make a drawing of what is to be turned.

- Cutting with the wrong lathe speed. First projects are normally spindle projects on smaller pieces of wood requiring greater RPM's to allow for smooth cutting. Slower is not necessarily safer. In bowl turning, starting

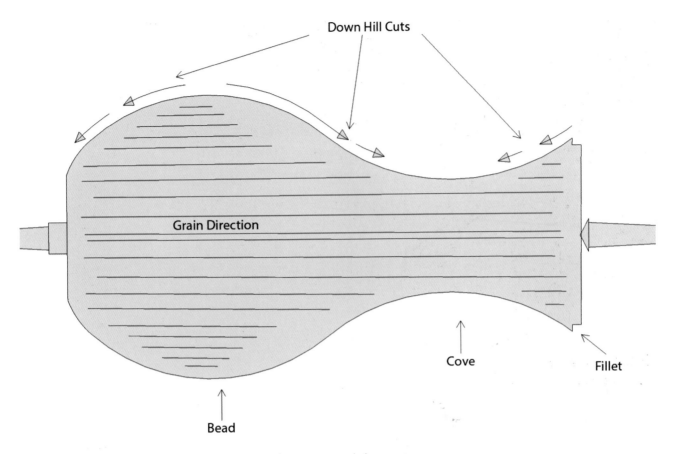

Down Hill Cuts

Grain Direction

Cove

Fillet

Bead

Downhill to the grain in spindle turning is always toward the center.

with out-of-balance stock may require the speed to be reduced to its minimum until the stock is more balanced; then the speed can be increased to improve the cuts. Cutting projects with voids or discontinuous surfaces also requires an increase in lathe speed for more cutting control.

- Working with dull tools. Everyone can recognize the improvement of the cut surface and the greater ease in cutting when a tool is sharpened, but few new wood turners recognize when it's time to resharpen a tool. If in doubt—sharpen. Sharpening requires a light hand to "dress the edge" rather than "grinding the tool."

- Not recognizing that you have to "pay your dues." Doing it again to improve lathe/tool/body operation is called "practicing," which few do enough. Make one project; examine what could have been done differently to improve; then do it again. Don't attempt

complex projects in quality wood without doing a prototype, as you may end up with disappointing results and waste good wood. Consider making a sample in plain wood first. Be sure to spend a lot of time with your spindle projects. These are the activities where the most is learned about tool usage and body movements. Don't skip the basics.

- Direction of cuts. When making cuts, we try to cut "downhill to the grain." This is the direction in which the fibers being cut are most supported by the uncut fibers. The supported fibers cut more cleanly, resulting in less tear out, smoother cutting and the final effect—less sanding. Cutting the other direction is like rubbing a cat backwards.

In spindle work, downhill to the grain is always towards the center of the spindle. In bowl turning, down hill changes direction depending on the blank's orientation. More about this later in the book.

Getting Started — Turning Between Centers

Objectives

- Introduce the student to the lathe operations.

- Learn the use of major spindle turning tools.

- Practice roughing out, planing, and cutting beads and coves.

- Learn about each tool as it is used.

- Practice cutting with feedback for position and movements.

- Introduce the A-B-C's of woodturning.

- Develop learner confidence while handling the basic cutting tools.

Discussion

Turning between centers (spindle turning) is the process of working with wood where the wood fibers are parallel with the axis of the lathe. In turning spindles the major cuts are the bead, cove and fillet.

Four of the major woodturning tools will be introduced in this section. Practice turning on spindle stock to develop the basic body, hand and arm movements and become more familiar and comfortable with the working of the wood lathe. Several projects are provided to introduce and expand spindle turning skills. If additional practice is desired additional activities are included in Appendix I.

Let's look at each of the major spindle turning tools.

The Spindle Roughing Gouge (SRG)

Description

The spindle roughing gouge is the first tool that most turners use and it is easy to develop skill and confidence with.

The "SRG" is named *spindle roughing gouge (Photo 1)* to indicate that this tool is not to be used for roughing out bowls or any hollowing applications! This misuse has led to many cases of serious injury.

The tool is typically ground straight across and with a bevel angle of about 45 degrees, optimizing it for turning round spindles from a square piece of stock. The tool can be rotated in order to use *all* the edge rather than just the portion in the center. This reduces the need to resharpen as frequently.

In furniture construction, a round chair leg may need to be cut against a square mounting shoulder. Here the tool is rolled up on its side to allow rounding the leg cleanly next to the square mounting shoulder.

What to watch out for

- New turners fail to hold the tool square to the work, which causes one shoulder of the tool to catch and run off in the opposite direction.
- Also, new turners fail to start the cut with the handle low enough to "rub the bevel" before raising the handle into the cutting position. Failing to raise slowly into a shearing cut position results in raising the handle too far and scraping the fibers away, rather than a controlled, easy slicing of the fibers.
- If the turner does not work toward the project end in a sweeping cut, the tool can potentially catch on one of the square corners at the end of the piece.
- Good body position requires the feet to be separated and the body weight transferred from one foot to the other as the cut progresses along the spindle. When the feet are held tightly together and the tool supported against the hip, the body is unable to smoothly advance the tool across the wood.
- Pressing the tool against the tool rest too hard can cause the tool to drag and jump during the cutting, requiring more effort and creating rougher cuts.

Activity

- Set the lathe speed to a moderately high speed (1,200–1,800 RPM).
- Place the spur drive in the headstock and the rotating live center in the tailstock.
- Mount the practice blank between these centers.

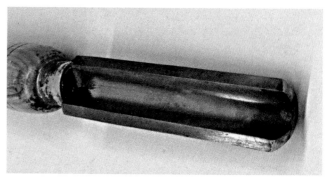

1. The spindle roughing gouge (SRG) is just for getting the spindle round.

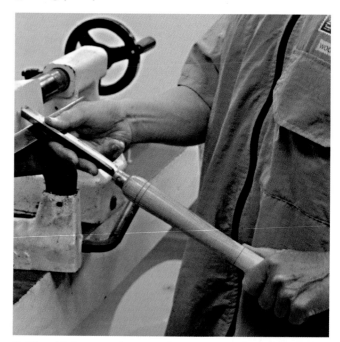

2. The SRG is ready to make a cut with the handle down and anchored.

- Place the tool on the tool rest squarely at 90 degrees to the work while holding the handle low and next to your body. (*Photo 2*)
- Examine the height of the tool rest and adjust it if necessary to allow the cutting edge of the tool to be a little above the center of the spindle and approximately ¼" from the spindle. When readjusting the tool rest, be sure to set it square to the spindle.
- Rotate the wood by hand to assure that there are no obstructions and the spindle is free to rotate.
- Turn the lathe on, stepping to one side "just in case."

- Place the tool on the tool rest with the flute facing upward and the handle against your side.
- To begin the cut, raise the tool handle and advance the tool until only the bevel *behind* the cutting edge is touching the wood. Nothing should be cutting at the point.
- Raise the handle a little until the wood fibers begin to be cut—stop raising the handle further. You are now in the correct cutting position.
- With the tool locked to your side, shift your weight from one foot to the other to advance along the tool rest.
- Work toward the end of the square practice stock and in successive cuts. Continue to work back toward the center.
- Switch hands and work the other end backward toward the center.
- Work smoothly back and forth until the spindle is evenly round and true.
- Leave the smoothed spindle on the lathe for use in the next activity.

The Skew Chisel

Description
The skew chisel is a double-beveled cutting tool with the cutting edge angled in one direction at about 70 degrees (skewed). *(Photo 3)*

Skew chisels are manufactured in different configurations from round or rectangular stock. The preferred shape for the tool has a flat edge on the long point side and a rounded edge on the short point side. As you will see, this configuration will facilitate the basic cuts we will learn.

There is a general preference for skew chisels made from rectangular stock, as they are stiffer and develop less vibration during cuts and are easier to sharpen.

A skew chisel of about ¾–1" in width is most flexible, from cutting beads to pen turning. Wider skews work better in roughing cuts and

3. Here are three typical skew chisels, one with a radiused edge.

planing cuts and on larger work such as Newell posts and chair spindles.

The length of the bevel should be 1½ times the thickness of the stock (shaft) and ground at a 70-degree angle to the shaft. The edge of the tool on the long point side (sometimes called the toe) should be square to allow for easy "V" cuts. The edge on the shorter point side (sometimes called the heel) should be rounded over to assist in rolling the tool during the cutting of beads.

On some skews the cutting edge is radiused with the first 20% of that edge starting from the long point perpendicular to the shaft to aid in better peel cuts. The balance of the edge then is rounded as illustrated above.

The skew chisel is your most versatile tool and is capable of many different uses. The basic cuts from which all skew chisel operations evolve are the planing cut, the peel cut, and the "V" cut.

Planing cuts
As with the bench plane for the cabinetmaker, the skew's planing cut levels and smoothes the wood surface, cleaning up a roughed out wood

4. Start the planing cut with the skew in this position, cutting toward the right.

spindle and flattening out ridges left by the spindle roughing gouge. Some shaping can also be done, creating positive curvatures in projects such as tool handles or wood pens.

For ease and comfort, the tool rest is raised so that the cutting edge rests against the spindle at about 11 o'clock. Remember to place the tool against the tool rest with the bevel resting against the spindle. Raise the handle slowly to bring the cutting edge into contact with the wood. Allow the handle to rotate slightly as the bevel comes into contact. *(Photo 4)*

As the handle is raised, the edge of the tool contacts the spindle surface and a small shaving begins to appear. *Do not raise the handle further.* Lock the tool to your body and move horizontally along the tool rest without changing your body or tool positions, transferring your weight from one foot to the other. If you move your hand slightly you will change the angle, and the cut will change.

If the wood surface is irregular or bumpy, only the highest surface will be cut and the lower portions will not be cut. Repeating this cut levels the surface until the entire surface is equally planed.

Peel cuts

The peel cut removes large amounts of wood rapidly but with some torn grain and an irregular surface. This cut is very safe to perform as long as the bite size remains small. The cut will have to be cleaned up later.

The tool is laid down flat on its side with the long point facing the wood, the tool's handle is raised, and the tool rolls into the wood. As the spindle diameter gets smaller the tool is advanced to maintain the cutting action.

If your skew is the style with a radiused edge and the first ¼ inch of the edge is ground horizontally, it will create a peel cut that will be flat and not as jagged. The tool used in this fashion can also be applied to cleaning up badly frayed areas or knots, if applied lightly.

"V" cuts

As the name implies, this cut creates a v-shaped groove in the spindle. The "V" cut is a very clean cut through the wood's end grain fibers, a quality not matched by any other tool. "V" cuts are used for layout lines, decorative cuts, or for parting deeply into the wood, as in cutting off the end of a tool handle cleanly.

The "V" cut is made by placing the tool vertically on the tool rest with the long point downward. To keep the tool perfectly vertical it is important that the flat edge rests squarely on your tool rest. The tool is then pushed into the wood with an arching motion. As the tool is advanced the tip will cut a small "V"-shaped groove. Further pressure on the tool at this point will not enlarge the groove, only burn the wood around it.

To expand the "V" cut the tool is moved slightly to the right or left and the long point set to cut a parallel groove no more than ¹⁄₁₆" further to the right or left. As the tool is advanced, the wood on the previously cut side of the tool will fracture off leaving a wider groove and a smooth wall surface. The tool is then placed on the opposite side of the original cut and the operation repeated as the "V" cut is enlarged.

Leaning the skew chisel to the right or left may cause the edge to catch in the wood and cut a spiral, ruining the wood surface. Sanding a "V" groove is never necessary.

Activity

Planing cut

- Raise the tool rest so that the skew chisel rests on the tool rest and touches the wood spindle at about 11 o'clock.
- With the lathe turned off, practice raising the tool handle until the bevel of the skew contacts the surface of the spindle. There will be a definite stop when the handle is raised far enough. Note that the tool also rotates in the hand slightly in order to maintain the contact. Also look at how the tool lies against the wood. The cutting edge should be about 45 degrees across the spindle fibers for the best slicing cuts, and never square to the spindle.
- Turn the lathe on and rest the skew chisel on the tool rest with the heel of the bevel resting lightly against the rotating spindle.
- Slowly raise the support hand until the faintest wisps of wood fibers appear at the cutting edge. *(Photo 5)*

- Lock your body into a firm position with each forearm anchored against your side.
- Advance the cut by transferring your weight from one foot to the other and not changing the position of the locked arms.
- Always advance toward the ends of the turning stock. At some point change hands and cut with the skew chisel facing the opposite direction.
- The cut surface should be smooth and shiny from the clean cuts.

"V" cuts

- With the skew chisel standing on its edge and with the long point facing downward toward the spindle, practice making several "V" cuts. *(Photo 6)*
- Remember, do not lean the tool, only fan the handle to the right or left to widen the cut.
- If the widening cut is more than 1/16" away from the initial cut, a new cut will be started and the initial cut will not widen. The distance between widening cuts must be small enough that the intervening material will fracture off out of the cut.
- Leave the spindle stock on the lathe for the continuation of the practice activity.

5. Skew chisel flat on the rest, long point facing the wood, ready to make a peel cut.

6. "V" cuts start with the long point down and the skew standing on its flat edge.

Parting Tools

Description

There are many different shapes of parting tools, all of which are designed to accomplish the same tasks—separating projects from their support, establishing dimensions, cutting fillets, or making tenons. *(Photo 7)*

1. The standard parting tool. The edge is square to the shaft and centered. Being a double-edged tool, it can cut equally well from either face. When using this tool, always make a pair of overlapping cuts to prevent the tool from binding in the wood.

2. The diamond parting tool. *(Photo 8)* The diamond shape allows only the cutting edge to be in contact with the wood. The rest of the shaft is relieved to reduce the possibility of the tool binding in the wood. Be sure to sharpen equally from both sides to keep the edge in the center.

Parting tools have a bevel below the cutting edge and are presented as a bevel rubbing cutting tool (e.g., rub the bevel, raise the handle to cut, and advance the tool into the cut). As the parted diameter gets smaller, the tool must be advanced forward into the wood to keep the bevel rubbing.

- Always allow clearance so the tool doesn't bind by making two overlapping cuts, progressing alternately between the left and right cuts. *(Photo 9)*
- I recommend having two parting tools, a thinner one (⅛" to ¹⁄₁₆") to part off projects and a wider one (¼" to ⅜") to cut tenons or make fillets.
- Longer handles on larger parting tools allow for more support of the cut and are very useful when doing a one-handed parting off cut.
- Practice parting off spindles one-handed, keeping the tool shaft against your forearm for better support and the other hand free to loosely support the project as it is separated.
- If you think you can't hold the parted off piece, don't try. Reduce the parted diameter and then cut the work free with a saw.

7. Parting tools come in many sizes and shapes.

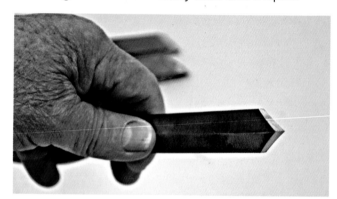

8. The diamond parting tool must keep the cutting edge in the center.

9. Parting tool cuts always overlap for safety.

- In parting off a spindle project, plan the work so that the parting off cut is near the headstock, not the tailstock. In this orientation, the work stops turning when parted off and doesn't fly away.

Activity
- Continue the practice activity by making several parting cuts with the parting tool along the spindle that was just smoothed out.
- Place the parting cuts about one inch apart and to a depth of about ½ inch. Use a ruler and pencil to mark out the one-inch separations for the cuts. A pair of calipers set to ½ inch can be used as a sizing gauge to check the diameter.
- Remember that each cut requires an overlapping relief cut to allow safe clearance for the tool.
- The tool is a bevel-rubbing tool. Remember to allow the tool to ride the bevel down into the cut.
- Save the wood for the next practice activity.

Shallow Fluted Gouge (Spindle Gouge)

Description
The shallow fluted gouge generally has a short handle and a small, shallow cross section. These features allow them to be easily manipulated for cutting beads and coves, cuts where the tool is held close to the spindle and vibration is limited.

Many shallow fluted gouges have the flute ground about half way into the round tool stock and some much shallower. Tools that have the flute ground shallower in the steel can be shaped into more severe bevel angles for use in detail work. These "detail gouges" can produce fine detail, but will also require more skill to manipulate.

There are three typical grinds *(Photo 10)*:
- Straight across (typically a factory grind).

- Slightly swept back to relieve the shoulders for more access to the work.
- Severely under cut and swept back, even pointed, to use in cutting very fine detail. Initially I suggest this grind be avoided, as it requires more control and user skill.

Cutting beads
Cutting beads *(Photo 11)* can be a challenging cut to learn. There are several body motions needed to keep the bevel in contact with the wood, as the surface of the work changes direction from

10. Three shallow-fluted spindle gouges are the traditional, swept back, and detail grinds.

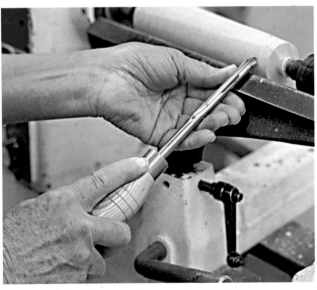

11. The starting position for a right hand bead places the index finger on top of the tool.

12. See that the lower side of the tool is doing the cut.

13. As the right hand bead continues, the tool rolls over to the right.

14. Completing the bead, the gouge is almost vertical to keep the edge cutting.

horizontal to vertical during the shaping of the bead. To keep the tool cutting properly, the handle is raised as the cut deepens, the tool is rotated to keep the bevel in contact with the wood surface and the handle is fanned outward. All three motions occur at the same time!

The bead is cut from left and right sides, working "downhill to the grain" from the bead's centerline toward either side. Cutting beads symmetrically is a challenge in order to get both sides identical. The solution is practice.

Before starting, place one hand on the handle with the index finger on top of the tool to allow unrestricted rotation of the wrist, the other hand pinching the tool shaft and supporting it at the tool rest.

With the flute of the tool facing upward, lift the handle until the cutting edge engages the wood surface and a shaving starts to be produced. *(Photo 12)*

- Slowly rotate the tool in the direction of the cut. The cut will always be on the downhill side of the tool. *(Photo 13)*
- As the curve of the bead increases, the tool needs to rotate further in order to keep the edge in contact with the surface being cut.

- As the bead is shaped, the handle of the tool must move outward from the bead to stay in continuous contact with the wood surface. *(Photo 14)*
- If you start to cut on the *uphill side* of the tool, you are turning the tool in the wrong direction. The cut is always on the downhill side of the gouge.
- Work slowly, keeping your eye on the wood surface to assure yourself that there is always contact between the bevel and the cut surface.
- When working in on the opposite side of the bead, the starting hand position should be adjusted to allow the wrist to move freely in the opposite direction.

15. Start a cove cut to the left with the tool engaging the left cutting edge.

16. Complete the cove with the gouge facing upward.

Cutting a cove

Cove cutting is a scooping cut which also requires a large movement to keep the cutting edge engaged in the wood. *(Photos 15 and 16)* The tool is started at the top of one side of the cove and cut to the center only. The completion of the cove is done from the opposite direction. Making the two halves match in the center requires some patience and practice.

- Start with the tool rotated toward the cut far enough so that the tool edge engages the wood.
- With a scooping motion, move the tool forward towards the cove centerline.
- As the center is approached the tool is rolled backward until the flute faces directly upward at the end of the cut.
- Repeat the action from the opposite side, stopping at the center with the flute facing upward.
- The next pair of cuts are started a small distance outward from the first set, increasing the width and depth of the cove.

17. Practice cutting beads, trying not to eliminate the pencil line until the last cut.

Activity

Turning beads

- Mount a practice blank and turn the blank round with the spindle roughing gouge. *(Photo 17)*
- Plane the blank smooth with your skew chisel, then add parting cuts about one inch apart with your parting tool. These steps may already have been completed in the preceding activities.

Turning beads with a shallow fluted gouge.

Mark the center of each one-inch section with a pencil.

- Begin turning a bead by resting the shallow fluted gouge on the spindle surface with the flute of the tool facing slightly to the left.
- Raise the handle until shavings begin to appear, then roll the tool over to the left, shaving off the left corner.
- Repeat the action facing the tool to the right and shaving off the right corner.

  Continue cutting, with the tool moved closer to the pencil mark, and a greater radius being cut on both left and right sides.
- As the bead becomes more pronounced the tool is rolled further each way so that the cutting edge can stay in contact with the wood surface, which, no longer horizontal, is becoming more vertical.
- As the bead takes shape, the handle of the gouge must also be moved laterally in order to allow the cutting edge to stay engaged with the wood surface, which is now almost vertical.
- Complete as many beads as are possible on the practice stock mounted. *(Photo 18)*

Turning coves

- Mount a new piece of practice stock on the lathe if needed. Round and smooth the stock as in the last activity.
- To start cutting the cove, the gouge is placed on the surface and rotated so that the leading (lower) edge begins the cut. Then the tool is advanced in the direction of the flute.
- The handle is unrolled so that the flute ends up facing vertically as the cut ends at the bottom of the desired cove. Repeat this action from the opposite direction, creating a small scoop shaped depression, similar to scooping ice cream.
- Each successive cut from the right and left sides begins a small distance further away from the scooped out area and ends in the center. As the cut deepens the gouge is pushed further forward to allow the cutting edge to stay engaged with the wood surface.

Repetition is necessary to develop skill

These activities require a *lot* of repetition in order to build manual dexterity and turning skills.

At the end of each practice activity, examine your work and the problems encountered, reread the steps, and try again until you feel comfortable and in control of the cuts.

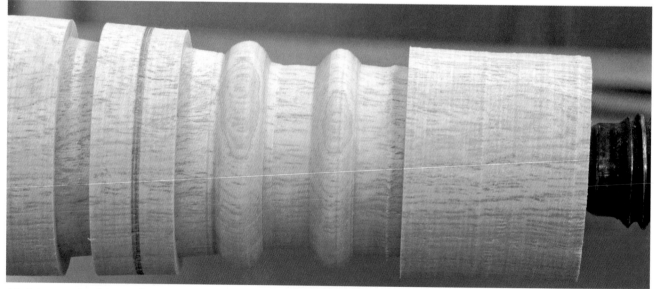

18. Practice beads are hard to make alike, but worth the effort.

2

Keeping Your Tools Sharp

Objectives

- Learn to sharpen the five basic tools.
- Develop skill at hand sharpening.
- Select the grinds and bevel angles for your tools.

Discussion

Purpose of sharpening

Wood is abrasive, some woods more so than others. As we work tools get less capable, and so we work harder, and the results show it. How can we tell when to sharpen our tools?

- We are working harder, pushing harder and getting poorer results.
- The finished surface becomes rougher, more ragged, and more torn grain shows up.
- Vibration increases as the tool "bounces" over the wood fibers and cuts less.
- Tools get warmer as they try to cut (partially due to us pushing harder).
- As we become more familiar with the *sound* of the cutting process, we find that the sound changes as the tools get dull.
- Assume that most new tools from the store are really a "kit ready for assembly" and will require some reshaping and sharpening.

Sharpening Station

There are several ways to maintain the cutting edge on your tools. Generally, a slow speed (1750 RPM) grinder equipped with aluminum oxide (Al_2O_3) wheels is preferred. The aluminum oxide wheels cut high-speed steel (HSS) cleanly and their surfaces are friable (they chip off), leaving sharp cutting edges. Most commonly used are two wheels: one wheel with 80 grit for scrapers and spindle roughing gouges, and one wheel with 120 grit for gouges and skews. Several grinders come with a gray carborundum wheel, which will not cut the tool steel and should be immediately replaced. The aluminum oxide wheel colors are codes to the wheel composition:

- White stones are aluminum oxide (Al_2O_3), most commonly with a friable surface which stays sharp.
- Blue stones are similar but with cobalt added for a harder surface. They are used where a lot of grinding is done.
- Pink stones are the hardest wheels, with chromium oxide added for additional hardness. They require more pressure to use and load most easily.

You will need a sharpening jig to allow you to accurately sharpen complex shapes, such as the fingernail profile on gouges, and you'll need a sturdy platform that can be easily adjusted to allow hand sharpening. An inexpensive industrial diamond wheel dresser will help you keep the sharpening wheels free of clogging metal waste and cutting more coolly *(Photo 1)*. Also a mono-crystalline diamond impregnated sharpening card for touching up edges (generally 600-grit) is handy.

As always, don't forget safety issues. Wear your safety glasses and a dust mask when dressing the wheels and sharpening your tools.

Sharpening Tools with Slow Speed Grinders

- Keep the sharpening wheels clean and running true, frequently using the wheel dresser to clean the surface of the accumulated gray matter. Sharpen with a light touch; we are only dressing up the edge, not grinding away metal. If the tool discolors, you may be applying too much pressure; lighten your touch and clean the grinding wheel.
- Mount your grinder near your lathe so you will be willing to go to it more frequently. It should be at about the same height as your lathe and equipped with a good light source.

1. An inexpensive diamond wheel dresser is necessary to keep the wheels clean.

2. Test a new wheel by ringing it. If it rings, it is good.

Safely Setting Up a New Grinder and Replacing a Wheel

- Test the wheels for soundness by removing them from the grinder, placing them on a wooden dowel and lightly tapping the edge with the wooden tool handle *(Photo 2)*. They should ring; if they don't, return them to the vendor as they are damaged and will be unsafe to use.

- Break in a new grinder or wheel by turning on the grinder for a few seconds, checking for vibration. If you encounter serious vibration, power down the grinder, loosen one wheel and rotate it 180 degrees. Retighten it and try it again to minimize the vibrations.
- True the wheels by placing your wheel dresser on the sharpening platform, and with a light touch remove the out-of-round vibrations. Be sure you have your dust mask in place, as the dust is bad for your lungs!

When Is the Tool Sharp?

- As you sharpen a tool look for sparks to start coming over the top of the cutting edge. This indicates that the final edge is near.
- When you are close, hold the tool to the bright light and see if you can see an edge. "If you can see the edge, there is no edge." Because there is a small flat area that is reflecting the light. When the edge is achieved there will be no glint reflected.
- Learn the feel of a sharp edge; it will catch in the folds of your fingerprint and cut paper easily.
- Keep the tool cool. If your tools are high speed steel (most newer tools are), the coloring will not damage the temper of the tool, but will indicate that you are using too much pressure or you have not cleaned the grinding wheel recently.
- Sharpen carbon steel tools very carefully. As soon as the tool colors you have lost the temper and the edge will not hold. Sharpen once lightly, dunk the tool in a glass of water, and then repeat the process until your edge is achieved.

Choosing the Sharpening Angle

When placing a tool on the grinding wheel the bevel should completely rest against the wheel face. Otherwise too much metal will be ground

3. This sharpening fixture is set too close to the wheel. See the felt marker?

4. The fixture is properly adjusted to fully align with the tool bevel.

away and too much time spent in the process. Jigs and fixtures simplify this realignment process by allowing the turner to repeat the same setting without loss of either time or metal.

In setting or resetting the fixture or grinder platform it may be helpful to color the tool bevel with a felt marker. Touch the colored tool against the wheel and check where the marker has been abraded away. *(Photos 3 and 4)*

When the marker is ground off high on the point, you must increase the sharpening angle; when ground low on the tool heel, reduce the sharpening angle until the full face of the tool shows a continuous light area. This is easy, quick and accurate.

Tool Use and Sharpening Information

Tools	Suggested Sharpening Angle	Comments	Process
Spindle roughing gouge	45°	• Corners of gouges should be kept square and not rounded over.	• Square the tool to the grinder, resting it on the sharpening platform. • Rotate the tool in only one direction to not over-sharpen the center.
Shallow fluted (spindle) gouge	30–40°	• Angle may be lower for beginners for better control. • A straight across grind works well for beginners. • Swept back grind (fingernail profile) adds versatility but increases the learning curve. • Traditional grind gouge is ground straight across.	• Generally use a fixture to maintain a repeatable angle. • Sharpen left, sharpen right, and then blend across the full tool face. • Sharpen like a spindle roughing gouge to maintain the square face.
Deep fluted (bowl) gouge	35–40° 50–55° 60–65°	• For normal bowl turning. • For deeper bowls. • For bottoms of really deep bowls.	• Use a fixture to maintain a repeatable angle. Sharpen left, sharpen right, and then blend across the full tool face.
Skew chisel	12° <20°	• For softwoods. • For hard woods. • The skew angle should be ~ 70°. • Generally the bevel is 1½ times the thickness of the tool. • Round over the short point (the heel) of the tool.	• Rectangular skews may be sharpened by adjusting the platform to the correct angle. • Radiused skews require rotating the tools to follow the curvature. • Skews also benefit from honing after grinding.
Parting tool	30–50°	• Keep the edge straight and 90° to the tool shaft. • If the tool is diamond shaped, keep the cutting edge exactly in the center of the tool.	• Sharpen by sliding the tool left and right without turning the tool handle to keep a square edge.
Bowl scrapers	70–80°	• De-burr the tool before sharpening with a diamond plate by stroking the top face against a belt sander (motor off).	• Grinding raises a burr, which aids in cutting. • Burrs can be replaced by de-burring and burnishing the edge at 5° with a hardened rod.

When sharpening the tool the goal is to quickly repeat the selected angle and return the tool to use. The specific angle for tools is debated, with some turners suggesting a specific "best" angle. I believe that the one that works for you is the "best" angle. As a general guideline I have included a table as a starting point; however you choose what is best for you.

5. To sharpen the SRG in a long arm fixture, use very light downward pressure.

6. A safer method is to hand sharpen the SRG.

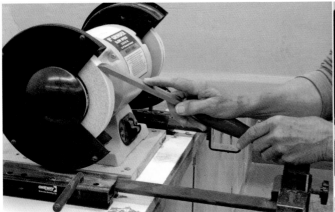

7a. Set the right face of a skew chisel using a "T" fixture.

7b. Set the opposite face from the other side of the "T."

Spindle Roughing Gouge Sharpening

Fixture method

The long "V" arm of most fixtures allows you to rest the tool handle in the fixture and rotate the tool against the wheel *(Photo 5)*. Be cautious of applying downward pressure while grinding as the arm could slip and the tool wedge into the face of the wheel, causing severe damage or injury.

Hand sharpening method

This tool can be sharpened by laying it flat on a grinder platform *(Photo 6)* with the platform adjusted so that the bevel is in contact with the grinder wheel; then manually rotate the tool to dress the complete edge. Assure that the tool is not over-rotated, which will cause the square shoulders to be rounded over.

Skew Chisel Sharpening

Fixture method— straight edged skews only

Rest the handle in either the left or right side of the "T" fixture *(Photos 7a and 7b)*, with the long point facing away and the cutting edge parallel with the wheel face. Adjust the arm length until the bevel rests against the wheel face evenly (try the felt marker method). Sharpen one face and repeat for the other side, keeping the cutting edge in the center of the tool body.

Hand sharpening method

Adjust the grinder platform to allow the bevel to rest flatly against the grinder wheel *(Photo 8)*. The tool is moved horizontally to create a straight, non-radiused edge. The tool is turned over and the same amount of grinding is done to the opposite side. This keeps the cutting edge centered in the tool. For skews with a curved edge, the turner must follow the curvature of the tool while moving the tool across the wheel face.

Skew chisels can be further sharpened by honing the edge *(Photo 9)*. A small 600-grit diamond pocket hone will do the task well. The hone is rested against the heel of the tool and the edge and lightly stroked on each face.

When the tool dulls many times, honing can quickly bring the edge back.

Sharpening a traditional grind gouge

Sharpening the traditional grind gouge is similar to sharpening the spindle roughing gouge. The tool is rested on the platform of the grinder, the platform is adjusted to match the bevel angle, and the tool is rotated slowly until the grinder has dressed the full bevel. *(Photo 10)*

Some may prefer to use the long "V" arm fixture to accomplish the same sharpening; however, it is a less secure method due to the fact that the long arm potentially can slip, or the gouge may become wedged between it and the grinding wheel.

Sharpening a Swept Back Shallow Fluted Gouge

Sharpening a gouge with a fixture

Sharpening the fingernail shape with a fixture provides quick repeatability of your initial grind and addresses the complex shape of the fingernail profile. There are many popular sharpening fixtures from North America, England and Australia; all contain the same basic features and functions. Adjusting the angle on the fixture sets the bevel angle and the length of the fixture arm determines the side shape. The tip protrudes through the fixture at a set length.

Once these settings are determined and locked, the fixture allows the wood turner to easily and quickly resharpen the tool to the same profile without wasting tool steel or time.

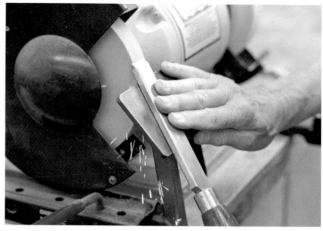

8. Hand sharpening a skew using a platform is safer.

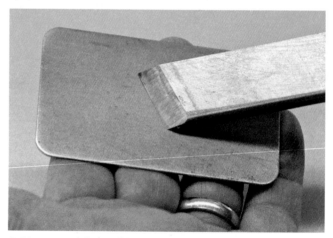

9. Honing a skew chisel after sharpening will improve the edge.

10. Sharpen a conventional grind gouge by rotating it against the wheel.

11. With a commercial fixture, set the tool projection.

12. Sharpen one side by sweeping the fixture to the right side.

Recently, some manufacturers have developed fixtures that restrict the undesirable sideways movement of the tool across the grinder wheel. This restriction prevents accidents associated with the tool sliding off one edge of the wheel while in the sharpening process. These fixtures allow for the same geometry as the older conventional fixtures.

To sharpen with a fixture, the tool is inserted into the fixture at a specified distance. *(Photo 11)*

The fixture is placed into its holder at a given distance from the grinding wheel surface. The sharpening starts with one side of the tool pressed lightly but firmly against the grinding wheel while raising and lowering the handle to create a radiused shoulder.

The other side of the tool is then completed in the same manner *(Photos 12 and 13)*. Lastly, the tool is rotated from one side over the tip and completely to the opposite side. This dresses the tip area, where there is less metal that needs to be ground away.

If the tip becomes too pointed, repeat this last step until the tip shape is what you require.

To prevent possible hand injuries, never place your hand between the fixture and the grinding wheel.

13. Sharpen the opposite side by sweeping in the opposite direction with the hand is on top.

14. Adjust the platform to match the gouge bevel angle.

15. Start the sharpening by rotating the tool and sweeping to the right.

16. This is the finishing position for the right hand side.

17. Free hand sharpening can also be done by pushing the tool upward while rotating.

Hand sharpening a swept back grind

Achieving the complex curve of the swept back wing and maintaining the grind angle while repositioning the handle of the tool is a set of complex motions that take time to learn. Therefore most beginning wood turners use a fixture. However, the reward is the ability to sharpen short or very small tools effectively. There are two techniques:

Using the grinder platform

Match the platform to the tip bevel angle. *(Photo 14)*

Start in the center of the tool with the tool resting gently against the wheel, and then fan the handle to the right while rotating the tool to keep the side bevel in contact with the wheel. *(Photos 15 and 16)*

Repeat the motion in the other direction.

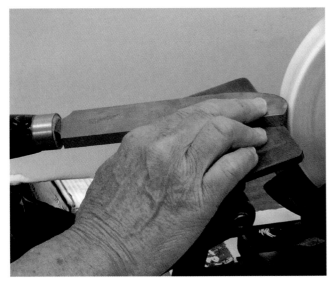

18. Sharpen a scraper by laying it on the platform and rotating it.

19. Parting tools start with the heel of the bevel against the wheel then raise the handle.

Free hand grinding method

The tool is held gently in the hand with the hand resting on the grinder platform and the bevel touching the grinding wheel face. The tool is rotated left or right while being gently pushed up the face of the grinding wheel *(Photo 17)*. The rotation is repeated in the opposite direction.

Sharpening Scrapers

Scrapers are easily sharpened by placing them on the grinder platform, matching the bevel angle to the grinding wheel and manually rotating the tool across the wheel. *(Photo 18)*

As the wheel cuts downward a small burr is pushed upward. The burr can be very sharp but short-lived.

Creating the burr can be aided by first assuring the flatness of the tool's top face. The tool can be flattened by laying its top face on an 80-grit belt sander (motor off) and stroking the scraper back and forth to re-square the top edge before sharpening.

Burrs can also be raised with a burnishing rod, shaft of a screwdriver, or bench chisel; all are hardened metal. The burnishing rod is pressed against the scraper's cutting edge at about a 5-degree upward angle. This will push up a small burr also.

Sharpening Parting Tools

Parting tools are also easily sharpened by hand by holding the tool gently against the grinding wheel with the heel of the bevel resting against the wheel *(Photo 19)*. Raise the tool until the tip of the bevel (the cutting edge) touches the wheel. Watch for sparks to come over the top edge of the tool. Repeat this action on the other face of the tool.

Be sure to keep the tool parallel with the wheel face so as not to round the tool edge. Diamond-shaped parting tools require that the edge remain exactly in the tool center.

3

Your First Projects

Objectives

- Introduce the use of a four jaw scroll chuck accessory.

- Apply basic cuts to a few simple projects.

- Add increasing complexity to the next project.

1. (above) A four jaw scroll chuck will be your first and most important accessory.

Activities

- Tool handles for simple screwdrivers.
- Bottle stoppers.
- Napkin rings.
- Bud vases.

Introducing the Four Jaw Scroll Chuck

The four jaw scroll chuck is the first and most important accessory for the wood turner. It provides a method to hold the project wood from only one end, allowing for work to be performed on the other end while mounted on the lathe. Actions such as completing a tool handle end, drilling a hole, or turning the interior of a bowl can be safely completed. Scroll chucks must be matched to your lathe's headstock thread. So when purchasing a chuck, the thread diameter and pitch of your lathe are needed to select the appropriate thread insert.

Scroll chucks operate by turning a key or operating two opposing levers that open and close four concentric jaws that securely hold the project at the exact center of the lathe. Most important in using a scroll chuck is making a matching tenon on the project wood to fit into the chuck's jaws securely. This tenon is cut to fit snugly into the chuck jaws while resting *on the top of the jaws* for maximum alignment and support.

There are two different styles of chuck jaws in use today: one uses a square tenon and another uses a dovetail-shaped tenon. Either style is acceptable.

Cutting square tenons

- The chuck pictured requires a square shouldered tenon so that the jaws bite evenly into the wood.
- Measure the internal diameter of the chuck jaws when they are partially closed, as is pictured. Transfer that measurement to the end of the project wood and pencil in a circle.
- Measure the *depth* of the chuck jaws and mark that dimension *minus $\frac{1}{16}$″* onto the side of the project wood. *(Photo 2)*
- Using your parting tool to remove all wood between the marks. *(Photo 3)*
- Examine the finished tenon to determine if the remaining shoulder is straight and the new smaller diameter is square to that shoulder. *(Photo 4)*

2. After transferring the measurements, this tenon is ready to be cut.

3. A square shoulder is important for a good, tight hold. Keep it straight.

4. See how the square shoulder sits tightly against the chuck jaw's top face.

5. Some brands of chucks require a dovetail shape to match their jaws.

6. Cutting a dovetail tenon can be easily done with a skew chisel and a peeling cut.

Cutting dovetail tenons

- Other manufacturers of chucks require that the tenon be cut in a dovetail shape to fit their chuck jaws. *(Photo 5)*
- Measurements are taken and transferred in the same manner as with the square tenon.
- Cut the tenon by laying a straight skew on its side with the long point facing the wood and away from the tailstock. *(Photo 6)*
- Complete a peel cut with the skew chisel to remove the wood between the pencil lines.
- Examine the resulting dovetail tenon to determine if its shoulder is square and the dovetail shape matches the chuck.

Using the chuck in the projects

Many of the following projects require access to the tailstock end of the work piece for drilling holes or parting off. To prepare for this activity, the four jaw scroll chuck is required. Prepare the stock as described earlier and add the required tenon to the tailstock end of the work piece for easier access.

7. A Jacob's chuck mounted to a Morris taper is a major accessory for drilling on the lathe.

Drilling with a Jacob's Chuck

When holes are drilled, the most accurate method is to use a Jacob's chuck mounted on a Morris taper *(Photo 7)* and fitted to your lathe's tailstock. The resulting hole will be centered and aligned in the project wood. This lathe accessory will also be very useful on many projects. However, for individuals not owning a Jacob's chuck, drilling on a drill press can be substituted. In this case move the project, still mounted in the four jaw scroll chuck, from the lathe to the drill press, align carefully, and drill the hole. Return the project and chuck to the lathe. The drilled hole may not be as perfectly centered as if drilled on the lathe.

Project: Tool Handles for Screwdrivers

Objectives
- Apply basic cutting skills to a simple project.
- Learn to mount a project in a four jaw scroll chuck.
- Learn to drill a hole using the lathe and a Jacob's chuck accessory.
- Complete a first project successfully.

Supplies *(Photos 8 and 9)*
- Hardwood stock 2" x 2" x 7".
- Inexpensive screwdriver.
- Coping saw to cut off the plastic screwdriver handle.
- Medium CA (cyanoacrylate or Super Glue) glue.
- Sandpaper.
- Turning Tools
- Spindle roughing gouge.
- Shallow fluted gouge.
- Skew chisel.
- Four jaw scroll chuck.
- Jacob's chuck and drills.

Discussion
While this activity easily dresses up an inexpensive, plastic-handled screw driver, it also introduces the new wood turner to the basic roughing and shaping activity. The four jaw scroll chuck and Jacob's chuck needed for drilling the hole are the two most required accessories to also become familiar with.

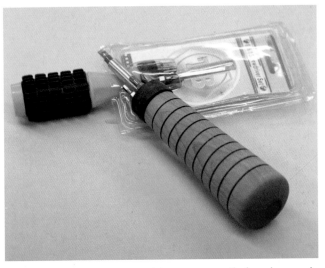

8. An inexpensive screwdriver can easily be dressed up with a custom handle.

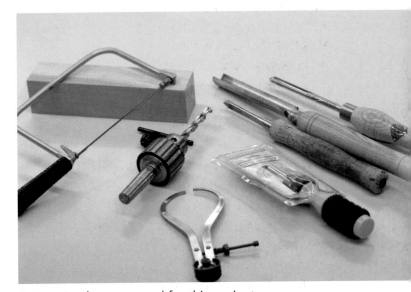

9. Here is what you need for this project.

10. Use a coping saw to cut away the plastic handle and free the metal.

Activity

- Purchase an inexpensive screwdriver at a local hardware store and remove the metal shaft by using a coping saw to cut off the plastic and remove the metal parts *(Photo 10)*. Most metal shafts will have small "ears" that will need to be ground away before completing the project assembly.

- Mount the handle blank between centers, set the lathe speed to 1200 RPM, and turn it round with the spindle roughing gouge (SRG).

- Add an appropriate tenon to the tailstock end of the project to fit your chuck using a parting tool or skew chisel and a set of calipers.

- Remove the handle blank and mount your four jaw chuck, being sure the chuck is secured tightly against the headstock.

- Remount the project by inserting the cut tenon into the partially closed chuck jaws, tightening the jaws while pressing the project wood into the chuck. Be sure the chuck jaws are well tightened.

- Set the lathe speed to 500 RPM. Drill a hole in the unsupported end of the handle blank using a Jacob's chuck and an appropriate drill bit selected to match the diameter of the screwdriver shaft *(Photo 11)*. Test fit the driver shaft to be sure of a snug fit. (The shaft will be glued in with medium CA glue at the end of the project.)

- Return the lathe speed to 1200 RPM and turn a pleasing shape that fits your hand stopping to occasionally test the fit to your hand. Add any decorations that you may want.

- Lower the lathe speed to approximately 800 RPM before sanding so you do not overheat the wood. Sand the project smooth using 80, 120, 180, and 220-grit sandpaper. Use each grit with the lathe running and the sandpaper constantly moving. Then sand with each grit with the lathe off and parallel with the wood grain until all visible circular marks are gone. Advance to the next grit and repeat the same sanding process. *(Photo 12)*

11. A Jacob's chuck with the correct drill easily centers the hole for the screwdriver shaft.

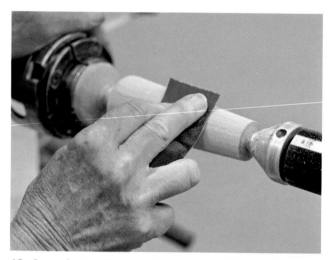

12. Completing the sanding on the lathe saves time and effort.

13. After completing the handle, part off carefully with a parting tool.

- Apply a finish of choice, being sure not to get the handle too slick as it will be harder to grasp.
- Part off the tool handle by using the skew chisel to make a series of "V" cuts at the headstock end near the chuck. As the cuts deepen the rotating handle will become unstable and will need to be held lightly while completing the cuts. Alternatively, reduce the diameter at the end of the handle to about ¼", stop the lathe, and cut the remainder through with a saw. *(Photo 13)*
- Sand and complete the end of the screwdriver.
- Mount the screwdriver shaft in the previously drilled hole using medium CA glue.

Alternate style project

If you buy a 4- or 6-way screwdriver *(Photo 14)*, you will have to remove a small metal collar from the plastic handle *(Photo 15)*. This component, into which the reversible shaft slides, must be mounted into the new handle first, and a smaller, centered hole must be drilled into which the shaft will later be fitted. Some screwdrivers will have a hexagonal collar that should be ground down to a round shape before the larger drill size is selected.

For the 4- or 6-way screwdriver:

- Measure the diameter of the collar removed from the plastic handle and drill a hole that allows for a snug fit. Drill the hole only as deep as the collar is long.
- Drill a smaller, centered hole to allow for the length of the screwdriver shaft to fit loosely into the handle.
- Test the fit of both components.
- Complete turning and finishing the tool handle as described for the first project.
- Glue the collar into place with medium CA glue.
- Insert the shaft to complete the project. *(Photo 16)*

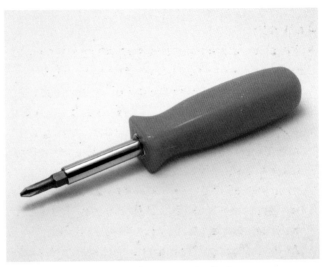

14. The six-way screwdrivers are a little more complex, but more functional.

15. Cutting the six-way screwdriver apart reveals the collar that must be mounted first.

16. A completed 6-way screwdriver becomes a dream to use as it fits your hand perfectly.

Project: Turning a Bottle Stopper

Objective

- To further practice bead turning, sanding and finishing techniques.
- To reduce the scale of the turning, which will require more delicate actions by the turner.

Supplies

- Hardwood stopper blanks 1½" x 1½" x 3".
- ⅜" hardwood dowels cut to 2-¼-inch length.
- Predrilled corks from a woodworking dealer.
- Jacob's chuck and a ⅜" drill bit for the dowel hole. See page 99 for draw bar/ collet chuck description and source.
- Yellow wood glue to glue in the dowels.
- A ⅜" collet chuck to hold the project for turning or, alternatively, a Jacob's chuck mounted in the headstock for the same purpose.
- Spindle roughing gouge.
- Shallow fluted spindle gouge.
- Sandpaper and finish.

Discussion

The bottle stopper activity introduces another means of holding projects on the wood lathe—the collet chuck. Many woodturners interested in continuing to make bottle stoppers may purchase an additional set of jaws for their scroll chucks designed for holding small dowels. The woodturning emphasizes controlled cutting of beads and/or coves. Remember to always keep the tail stock in place for additional support as long as possible. When it is removed to complete the stopper top light, delicate cuts should be employed with a recently sharpened tool.

17. Bottle stoppers are made from small scraps of collected hardwoods.

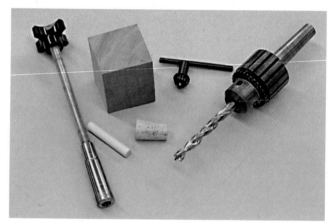

18. A ⅜" drill, dowel, and collet chuck are ready to start a stopper project.

Collet chuck and draw bar

The collet chuck is an inexpensive accessory for use with dowel mounted projects. It is assembled from a ⅜" bore machine collet, a piece of ⅜" all thread, and a ⅜"-20 commercial knob. The all thread is cut to length for your lathe and the knob and a washer are added. See page 99 for the source.

Activity

Prepare the stopper blanks by drilling a centered ⅜" hole in the project wood 1" deep. Glue a 2¼" long x ⅜" dowel using wood glue and allow to dry completely, preferably overnight.

- Mount the stopper blank into the lathe *(Photos 19 and 20)* using a draw bar and a ⅜" collet chuck or a Jacob's chuck. If you use a collet chuck assembly, place a collet chuck into the lathe's headstock, attach a locking knob to the outside of the headstock's hand wheel. Insert the stopper blank/dowel into the collet and tighten the draw bar until the dowel is secure.
- Always advance the tailstock for additional support during the initial steps of rough turning and shaping.
- Set the lathe speed to approximately 1,200 RPM and turn the desired shape (see following ideas for possible shapes).
- Remove the tailstock and carefully complete the end by keeping the cut very light and applying little cross-lathe pressure.
- Sand and finish the stopper.
- Remove the stopper from the lathe by loosening the draw bar and tapping the draw bar to free the collet from the lathe headstock, thus loosening the stopper's dowel.
- Add a drilled cork stopper and glue into place with yellow glue. Trim the dowel flush with the end of the stopper and sand it flat if necessary.

Some shape considerations
(Drawing 21)

- The base of the stopper should be larger than the diameter of the cork to be more attractive.
- The top of the stopper should have a "handle" to grab for easy removal when it is used.
- Keep the shape simple.

19. A blank with a dowel glued in is being inserted into the collet chuck.

20. Mount the blank on the lathe by tightening the collet chuck into the headstock taper.

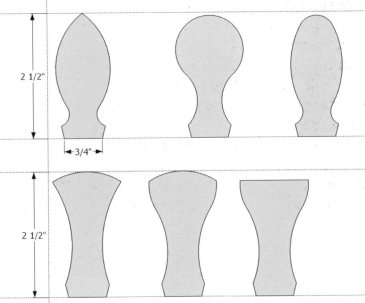

21. Here are a few stopper samples.

Project: Turning a Napkin Ring Set

Objectives
- Complete a more complex project.
- Transfer dimensions to a project.
- Shape a set of matching rings with similar characteristics.

Supplies
- Hardwood 3" x 3" x 9".
- Sandpaper 80, 120, 180, 220-grit.
- Shellac or oil varnish finish.
- Spindle roughing gouge.
- Parting tools and calipers.
- Four jaw scroll chuck.
- Shallow fluted gouge (spindle gouge).
- Skew chisel.
- Jacob's chuck and 1½" Forstner bit.

22. Napkin Rings make an elegant project and raise your skills at the same time.

Discussion

The dimensions for this project can be varied without difficulty if the concept and the proportions are maintained and the parting cut between the rings is *smaller in diameter* than the final Forstner bit hole drilled through the end. The rings require little decoration when the figure of the wood in very attractive. Decoration can be added to the rings with the tip of the skew chisel by making small "V" cuts on the surface or adding a small bead to each surface.

A burning wire accessory for decorations can be made from a short length of steel wire attached to two handles. The wire is placed on

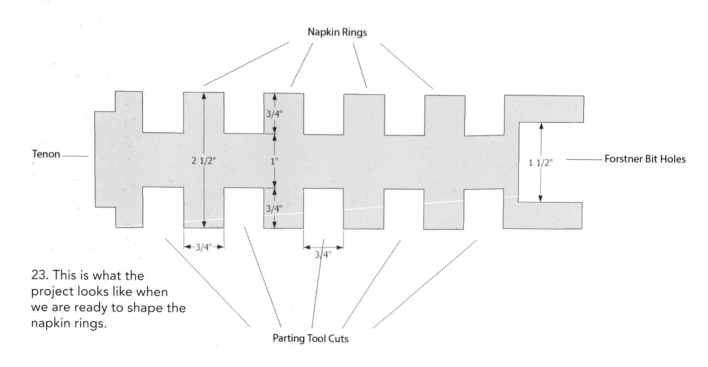

Napkin Rings

Tenon

3/4"

2 1/2"

1"

3/4"

3/4"

3/4"

1 1/2"

Forstner Bit Holes

Parting Tool Cuts

23. This is what the project looks like when we are ready to shape the napkin rings.

top of the project into a "V" groove and the lathe speed is increased. The wire causes friction and a burned area results. This process also raises the grain, which must be resanded before finishing the project.

Never hold the wire with your fingers.

It is important to completely sand the interior of the parted-off ring so that napkins can smoothly slide in and out. Generally an outside diameter (OD) of 3" and an inside diameter (ID) of 1½" are acceptable. Drawing 23 represents the concept of this project.

24. Lay out the dimensions with calipers and a pencil.

Activity

- Prepare stock by mounting the project wood between centers, setting the lathe speed to approximately 1800 RPM and making the project stock round with a spindle roughing gouge.
- Add a tenon appropriate for your four jaw chuck and remount it into the chuck. Bring up the tailstock for additional support and re-true the blanks if necessary.
- Mark out the napkin rings and separation areas *(Photo 24)*. The napkin rings will be ¾ inch wide followed by a separation area of ¾ inch to allow for later sanding of the edges. Mark out the first ring, then an area for a parting cut, and then the second ring, etc. Darken the separation areas with a pencil.
- Reduce the diameter between the napkin rings by using your parting tool and calipers to make the darkened separation area 1" in diameter. *(Photo 25)*

  Shape the napkin rings by first marking the napkin rings into thirds with a pencil. Roll a bead on the outer edges of the three rings with a shallow-fluted gouge, working only to the lines. Complete the bead by working back to the centerline. *(Photo 26)*

25. Reduce the waste wood between the rings to one inch.

26. Note the layout lines added before beginning to shape the first ring.

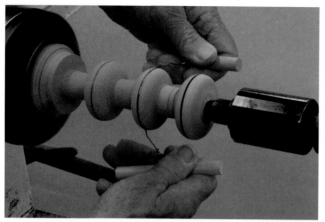

27. A burning wire placed in a small groove adds a nice decorative effect.

28. When drilling off the rings one at a time, use slower drilling speeds.

29. After the first ring is cut off, stop the lathe and retrieve it.

30. Clean up the interior by hand sanding.

- Sand the top and sides using 180- to 320-grit sandpaper. Decorative burn lines can be added by marking the center of the rings with the tip of a skew chisel first to create a small groove.
- Remove the tool rest and with a small steel wire attached to hand-made handles, burn in decorative marks *(Photo 27)*. The wire is placed on top of the "V" groove and pressure is applied until the wood smokes. Resand with 220-grit sandpaper to remove the surface debris formed.
- To separate the rings, mount a Jacob's chuck in the tailstock with a 1½" Forstner bit installed. Lower the lathe speed to 500 RPM and advance the tailstock quill to drill through the first napkin ring. Drill slowly as heat will be created. *(Photo 28)*
- When the first ring is drilled free, stop the lathe and remove it. Advance the tailstock and repeat the drilling steps until all rings have been freed. *(Photo 29)*

31. The completed napkin ring set is ready to use.

- If a portion of the wood is not cleanly removed by drilling, a pocketknife can quickly remove the waste. Sand the inside through all grits to 320-grit. *(Photo 30)*
- Add a finish to suit. *(Photo 31)*

Project: Bud Vase

Objectives
- Continue to practice transferring dimensions.
- Practice turning to the drawing dimensions.
- Develop skill in the transition between a bead and a cove.
- Practice drilling and flaring the end grain neck (an end grain cutting technique).

Supplies
- Hardwood blank 3" x 3" x 8".
- Sandpaper and finish.
- Tools.
- Four jaw chuck.
- Spindle roughing gouge (SRG).
- Shallow fluted gouge.
- Drill bits and Jacob's chuck.
- Parting tool and calipers.

Discussion
This apparently simple project includes activities that will come into constant use in woodturning. Furniture makers must make legs, backs and stretchers in sets that match. Transitioning from the cove of the vase neck to the bead shape of the body requires the student to reverse the rotation of the gouge as it moves from one shape area to the other. Work carefully while addressing the smoothness of the curve, eliminating any flat spots.

Note that this project is not designed to hold water and can only be used with dry or synthetic flowers.

32. The bud vase or dry flower pot project may not hold water, but still can be attractive.

Activity
- Set the lathe speed to 1800 RPM and prepare the project blank by mounting the wood between centers and turning it round. Add a chuck tenon to the tailstock end and remount it into your four jaw chuck. Bring up the tailstock for support and re-true the blank if required.
- Mark major sections of the blank from the drawing, being sure to place the top of the vase at the tailstock end of the blank. (Photo 33)

33. Lay out the vase lengths from the tailstock end.

34. Lay out the vase diameters with your parting tool and calipers.

- Mark the diameter and location of the narrow top onto the tailstock end of the blank, the location and diameter of the smallest and largest areas onto the body, and the location of the base of the vessel.
- Transfer the major diameters from the drawing using calipers and a parting tool with overlapping cuts *(Photo 34)*. Also place a shallow parting cut to mark the bottom of the vase.
- Beginning at the tailstock end of the lathe, shape the coved neck area and the top portion only of the matching bead section *(Photo 35)*. Do not shape the bottom (headstock end) of the vase until after the following steps in order to maintain the maximum mass and support.

- Set the lathe speed to 500 RPM and drill a hole from the tailstock end with the Jacob's chuck *(Photo 36)*. Select a drill bit that leaves at least a ¼" wall thickness in the neck area.
- Return the lathe speed to 1800 RPM and flair out the inside of the neck by using the spindle gouge, cutting from the center toward the rim *(Photo 37)*. The tool should have its flute facing 45 degrees towards the turner. Use light cuts with the tip of the tool only.
- Complete the shape by reducing the base diameter to a final dimension. *(Photo 38)*

35. Shape the neck portion only.

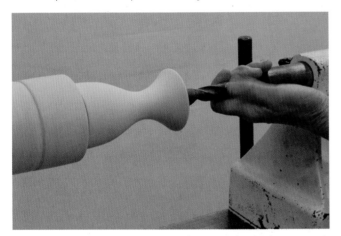

36. Drill the interior hole by slowing the lathe speed first.

37. Flair out the neck with a shallow fluted gouge from the center outward.

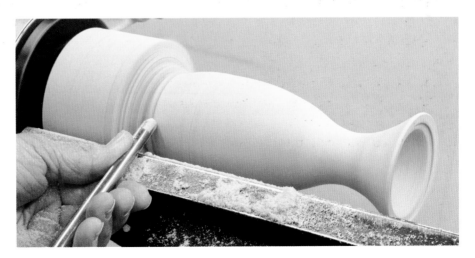

38. Now you can complete the final shaping of the base.

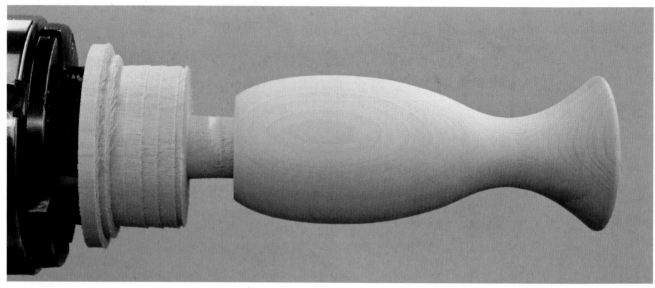

39. Reduce the diameter of the base to check the correctness of the curve, then part off.

- Sand as in the earlier projects with all grits from 80-grit to 220-grit and add an appropriate finish.
- Part off using your parting tool, making two overlapping cuts *(Photo 39)*. You may also choose to cut the final portion with a sharp pull saw.

40. Here is a drawing of the vase with dimensions.

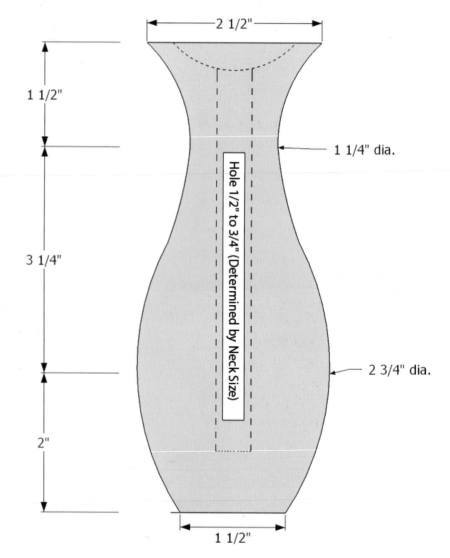

2 1/2"

1 1/2"

1 1/4" dia.

3 1/4"

Hole 1/2" to 3/4" (Determined by Neck Size)

2 3/4" dia.

2"

1 1/2"

4

Introduction to Faceplate Turning

Objectives

- Learn the basic steps for turning a bowl.
- Learn about the basic tools used in faceplate (bowl) turning.

1. (above) Simple first bowls.

Introduction

Turning cross grain bowls requires a different set of tools and actions. The primary tools used are the deep fluted gouge (bowl gouge) and the interior bowl scraper. The motions are more dramatic and require a large body movement. In many of the cuts the tool is only supported by the hands, arms, tool rest and bevel rubbing the wood surface.

There is a greater potential for injury to the lathe operator when turning wood bowls as the beginning cuts may be on larger, unbalanced wood blanks. The potential of the wood to separate from the lathe or for large pieces to fly off demands the use of the full face shield during all portions of the external bowl shaping. Do not rely on eye protection alone!

The Deep Fluted Gouge (Bowl Gouge)

The deep fluted gouge *(Photo 2)* is easily distinguished from the shallow fluted (spindle) gouge by a longer handle and blade as well as the deeper, more massive flute. This shape allows the tool to be used farther over the tool rest with less vibration potential than the shallower spindle gouge, making it ideal for turning bowls.

Out of the box the tool may be ground with a traditional straight-across grind or a fingernail profile. The latter tool profile is preferred for its greater flexibility, allowing the tool to do pull cuts and shear scraping. The fingernail profile is also called the Ellsworth, O'Donnell, or Irish grind. The length of the side grinds, whether straight or radiused, and the bevel and side angles, are all a matter of personal preference.

Tool Shape

When you buy a new tool, don't assume that it is usable until you sharpen it. Direct from the store the shape is normally for presentation only and is not sharp.

The bevel angle controls the ability of the tool to stay in contact with the surface while the cut is being made. The deeper the bowl, the blunter the tip bevel angle required to keep "rubbing the

2. Sweptback and traditional grind bowl gouges are both useful in bowl turning.

bevel." Generally a tip bevel angle of about 35 to 40 degrees covers most bowl turning activities while shorter bevel angles are reserved for making final cuts into deep bowls.

Interior Bowl Scrapers

Scrapers are a real workhorse tool *(Photo 3)*. They are used to:

- Finish cutting bowl interiors where the gouge becomes difficult to use,
- Complete surface smoothing prior to sanding,
- Make minor shape corrections to a project,
- Perform the primary cutting in hard, dense materials and plastics, or
- Hollow-in narrow, deep, or closed projects.

3. Bowl scrapers need to be big and heavy.

Most scrapers used in woodturning are ground with a bevel angle of about 10 to 15 degrees. When sharpening a scraper on a grinder, a burr is pushed upward. This burr can be left or removed depending on your needs. For softwood the burr is retained. The thickest scraper that will fit into the project dampens vibration and stabilizes the tool best because of its mass, so big is better.

You may eventually have a collection of scrapers that will match the curve of specific shapes. Some scrapers have a tear drop cutter that can be rotated to match different curves and a rounded shaft to allow the tool to be rotated to make clean shearing cuts.

With few exceptions scrapers should be used with the handle raised and the blade trailing to the project centerline to prevent catches. This requires raising the tool rest. Rotating the tool rest into the bowl gets the cutting edge closer to the wood surface and adds to stability. This helps make smoother cuts.

Holding a scraper with one side raised off the tool rest is very risky. If a deep cut occurs and the scraper catches, the raised edge may be slammed down onto the tool rest with your finger in-between.

Negative Rake Scrapers

Negative rake scrapers are ground with a compound angle created by adding an additional 5-degree bevel to the scraper's top surface. This extra angle allows the tools to be presented straighter into the wood, while reducing the potential to catch on the wood fibers. The tool doesn't retain a sharp cutting edge very long and is usually only used for smooth final cuts on hard woods.

Turning a Bowl

Bowl turning requires three different mountings of the blank as we proceed through the turning of the exterior, the interior, and finally the foot. In the first project we will use a screw chuck for the initial mounting and a "jam chuck" to complete the foot of the bowl. In future projects, other mounting methods will be presented.

Cutting "downhill to the grain" requires some thinking as the grain direction appears differently depending on whether you are inside or outside the bowl. Working on the outside, try to cut from the smaller diameter of the foot toward the larger diameter of the rim (*Drawing 4*). Inside it is the opposite, cutting from the rim toward the bottom or outside toward the middle.

Using the bowl gouge effectively

Always point the flute of the deep fluted bowl gouge in the direction of the cut. The shavings should come from the lower half of the tool, not the top portion. The tool is rotated to keep the bevel and cutting edge in contact with the surface, providing support and stability. Over-

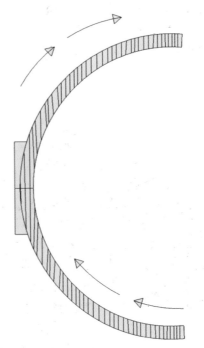

4. The cut direction on bowls is foot to rim outside and rim to foot inside.

rotating the tool exposes too much cutting edge and will cause the tool to grab a lot of wood at once, leading to a dig in or "catch." Also remember that, whether turning green or dry wood, all wood is abrasive to the sharp cutting edge. Resharpening the gouge frequently will get a good clean cut.

Getting the surface smooth on a rough blank

Many beginners place the tool bevel against the irregular surface and attempt to remove the irregularities. Since the surface is irregular, the tool tends to follow the pattern of the surface and the blank is not easily smoothed. The tool must be firmly held on the tool rest, the cutting edge only allowed to cut the most irregular, protruding wood fibers. Allow the wood to come to the tool and cut itself. Early in the rough shaping it may be a process of cutting wood, then air, then wood, etc. Cutting near the tip of the tool takes only small cuts and is easier to control at the beginning of the process.

Lathe speed

The speed of the lathe is very important: Too fast and the blank may fly off or the lathe may dance around the room; too slow and the tool cuts poorly. As the blank is brought into round, the lathe should be sped up, keeping its rotation slightly below the vibration point. Start at a lower speed, generally about 500 RPM, and increase the lathe speed as the bowl blank comes into balance.

Three Basic Steps in Bowl Turning

Turn the exterior (Drawing 5)

Cuts are made from the tailstock towards the headstock, balancing the blanks and shaping the curve of the bowl. A tenon is cut into the tailstock end of the blank, suitable for your chuck. Finally the exterior shape is completed.

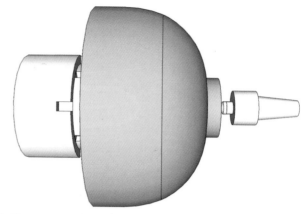

5. Phase one: Rough out the exterior and add a tenon.

6. Phase two: Hollow out the interior while the bowl is mounted in a scroll chuck.

Turn the interior (Drawing 6)

The rough-shaped bowl is reversed into the four jaw scroll chuck and the exterior is recut to correct any out-of-balance issues. As the bowl blank is made more round and balanced, the lathe speed can be increased in order to make smoother, cleaner cuts. Finally remove the interior of the bowl with successive cuts matching the shape of the interior and exterior and maintaining a constant wall thickness throughout.

Turn the foot (Drawing 7)

After the interior is completed, the bowl must be reversed again to complete the foot and bowl bottom. The first step of remounting the bowl is to create a jam chuck, a rounded piece of wood mounted into the four jaw scroll chuck and used to center and hold the shaped bowl while the foot

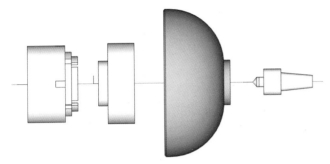

7. Phase three: Make a second reversal to complete the foot.

is completed. The bowl is placed over the jam chuck and the tailstock is brought up to apply supporting pressure. Then the bottom is shaped to completion. At the end, the bowl is removed from the jam chuck and the remaining small area under the tail stock live center is removed and hand sanded.

Mastering the External Bowl Cut

The Rule of 45's
Proper positioning of the body and gouge for exterior cuts is important to best support the tool, reduce body fatigue and generate the most controlled cuts. In general this comes down to the Rule of 45's.

- The tool rest is set across the blank at a 45-degree angle to the lathe bed.
- The gouge is held with its handle held downward at 45 degrees, with the handle against the turner's hip.
- The flute of the gouge is rotated at 45 degrees and faces the direction of the cut.

Mastering the Interior Bowl Cut
New turners need to master the interior bowl cutting technique. This technique positions the cutting edge and tool bevel in the proper location for beginning the cut, and rotates the tool through the shaping and finishing with the edge always in a safe position. To start, the cutting edge must be vertical to the uncut surface and the arm and wrist extended well behind the ways of the lathe. If you over-rotate your wrist

at the beginning of the cut, then allow your hand to come forward into a more natural and comfortable position. The tool will also rotate naturally in order to maintain the proper cutting position. This skill takes practice until it becomes a natural movement.

The steps in the cutting process are: **right hand push, right hand pivot, left hand push** (*Drawing 8*). These motions are combined with a rotation of the right wrist between the first and second movements.

Right Hand Push (*Photo 9*) This position engages the tool edge with the bowl surface and establishes a shoulder to support the tool as it cuts downward into the interior of the bowl.

The bowl gouge handle is held at a 45-degree angle *behind* the lathe bed with the flute positioned to face vertically. To check this, note that the bevel of the tool is parallel with the outside surface of the bowl. The turner's right hand grasps the tool in an extreme clockwise rotation with the wrist in an over-rotated position. The left hand is stationary on the tool rest, clamping the tool in position.

The edge of the gouge is placed against the bowl interior and the right hand pushes the tool into the bowl. The edge catches a small shoulder

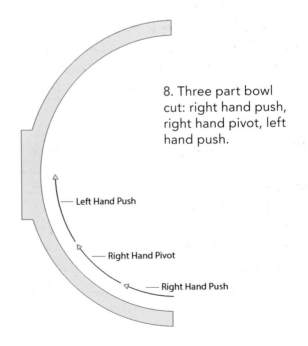

8. Three part bowl cut: right hand push, right hand pivot, left hand push.

Left Hand Push

Right Hand Pivot

Right Hand Push

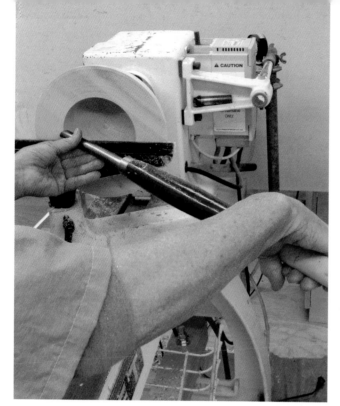

9. Phase I—Right Hand Push: The starting position is with the wrist over-rotated and the cutting edge vertical.

10. Phase II—Right Hand Pivot: The right hand comes forward while the wrist unrolls.

and the cut proceeds downward. When the tool cannot proceed further, the operator moves to the second part of the cut.

Right Hand Pivot (*Photo 10*) This action creates the bowl's interior curve.

Without releasing the initial grip, the right hand pulls forward to a position parallel with the ways of the lathe; at the same time the wrist rotates into a more natural and comfortable forward position. The left hand remains stationary, pivoting the tool against the tool rest. The tool has now rotated approximately 45 degrees, with the flute facing about 2 o'clock. As the tool moves farther into the bowl, the cutting edge is always in the correct position to slice through the wood fibers.

Left Hand Push (*Photo 11*) The right hand remains stationary and parallel with the ways and the left hand pushes the tool away from the operator and removes fibers from the center of the project.

During this portion of the cut, the tool moves horizontally across the bottom of the bowl in a relatively flat cut. The flute is still facing 45 degrees to the wood fibers.

11. Phase III—Left Hand Push: With the right hand parallel to the lathe, the left hand pushes forward.

By using this technique, the turner is freed from having to remember to rotate the tool to a different cutting position and can be assured that the tip will never cut too deeply into the bowl fibers and create a "catch."

The technique can be modified to make a more rounded bowl bottom by continuing to pull the right hand forward during the third phase left hand push. This pivots the tool around the left hand and creates a rounded bottom.

When planning your first bowls you may wish to consider two primary classical shapes.

Bowl Shape

When planning your first bowls you may wish to consider two primary classical shapes.

Continuous positive curve *(Drawing 12)*
This is the traditional bowl shape with no straight lines, a continuous curve, and no sudden changes in curvature and foot to "lift" the bowl off the resting surface.

Ogee curve *(Drawing 13)*
This is a more elegant shape in which there is one reversal of the curve direction, adding lightness to the top and interest and movement to the bowl. In attempting this shape be careful not to use two curve changes, as that may become confusing to the eye!

Sung Dynasty ceramic bowl *(Photo 14)*
This form has endured for centuries as it represents a shape that is pleasing to the eye and the hand. It has a continuous positive curve and a foot that supports and lifts the bowl.

12. Try for a continuous positive curve with no flat areas—a basic bowl shape.

13. An ogee shaped bowl has one curve reversal near the top or foot.

14. The Sung Dynasty rice bowl is a 3,000 year old classic shape.

5

Turning Your First Bowl

Objectives

- Learn the steps in mounting, turning and completing a dry wood bowl.

- Learn more about the differences in grain direction between bowls and spindles.

- Learn to use the deep fluted gouge.

- Learn to use the interior bowl scraper.

1. (above) Here is a simple bowl with a small ogee curve.

Supplies

- 9" x 9" x 4" dry wood bowl blank, such as poplar, maple, or another species. Sized to fit your lathe.
- 3" x 3" x 4" scrap wood for jam chuck.
- ⅜"–½" deep fluted gouge (bowl gouge).
- Parting tool.
- Four jaw scroll chuck with wood screw chuck (supplied with the chuck).
- Power drill and bit to fit the screw chuck's dimension.
- 1½" bowl interior scraper.
- Bowl wall thickness calipers.
- Face shield.

Discussion

Bowl turning is more dangerous than turning spindles between centers. The possibility of injury is increased. Therefore a full face shield should be worn at all times. Lathe speed should be carefully monitored to assure that a safe operating speed is not exceeded. If the lathe vibrates or moves, the speed is too great—reduce it until the wood is brought into balance.

Activity

Prepare and mount the blank

- It is desirable to create a roughly round shape on the band saw or by hand. This allows the blank to run as smoothly as possible when mounted on the lathe.
- Next find the exact center of the trimmed bowl blank and mark it on both sides. On the face side, drill a ⅜" hole, 1" deep to mount the screw chuck. Note that some screw chucks may require a different size hole. Check the manufacturer's literature.
- Set the lathe speed to 500 RPM, and mount the four jaw scroll chuck on the lathe headstock. Insert the screw chuck between the jaws and tighten securely. Measure the outside diameter of the closed chuck jaws and record that measurement for use in a later step.
- Screw the blank onto the mounted screw chuck until the blank's face rests on the face of the scroll chuck jaws *(Photo 2)*. This is important for a tight hold while turning. Bring up the tailstock and secure it for additional support.

Turn an exterior rough shape

- Using your deep fluted gouge, turn a pleasing bowl shape beginning at the tailstock end and working toward the headstock. Remember that the flute of the bowl gouge always points in the direction of your cut: tailstock toward headstock. As the balance of the bowl improves, the speed of the lathe can be increased in steps. Remember to use the Rule of 45's. *(Photo 3)*

2. Mounting the blank on a screw chuck is a good starting position.

3. The rule of 45's is gouge handle down at 45°, tool rest rotated 45°, and the gouge flute rotated 45°.

4. Begin to shape the exterior with the tailstock added for support.

5. Square up a tenon with the parting tool.

6. Here is the completed rough exterior ready to reverse into the scroll chuck.

Complete the exterior of the bowl

- Complete rough turning the exterior shape *(Photo 4)* from base to rim or tailstock end toward the headstock end. When the tool is in position against your body, you will have to move your body in a circular motion transferring your weight from the right foot to the left foot during each cut. If the cut exceeds your reach, stop the cut, reposition your body, and then resume the cut from where you left off.

- Transfer the chuck jaw measurement taken earlier above to the tailstock side of your rough bowl and turn a tenon *(Photo 5)* to that diameter. It will be sized to fit the interior of the chuck jaws for clamping. After cutting the tenon, the exterior may need reshaping to account for the wood lost in creating the tenon and defining the bowl's foot.

- When cutting the tenon, remember that all tenons require a flat onto which the chuck jaws will rest, providing support for the blank. The length of tenon should be slightly shorter than the depth of the chuck's jaws so that it rests on the top of the jaws, not on the bottom.

  Unscrew the bowl blank from the screw chuck, remove the screw chuck and reverse the bowl into the chuck jaws. After tightening the chuck thoroughly *(Photos 6 and 7)*, you may need to touch up the bowl shape, as any change in mounting may not provide perfect realignment.

  After the exterior clean up, sand the exterior to final grit.

Turn the bowl interior
using the three part bowl cut

- Starting in the center, turn a small bowl shape and work outward and downward until the wall thickness of about 1" is established. The wall thickness should be measured with bowl calipers to assure the constant wall thickness throughout. Be cautious and not allow the center to get thinner than the same wall thickness.

- Begin to work the wall thickness to the final dimension in 1" increments *(Photo 8)*. Work down 1" only, checking your measurements as you go. Smooth the final surface. During the first one-inch, assure yourself that the bowl's rim is completed since you can't easily go back to it later.

- Move down another inch, turn the wall to the same thickness and blend the two surfaces together. Always assure that the walls are of a uniform thickness, using calipers to measure frequently as you go.

- When you get to the bottom be sure that the bottom curve of the bowl is shallower than the thickness of the walls to allow shaping of the foot at the next step. *(Photo 9)*

- Sand the interior to final grit and add finish.

7. Mount into the chuck using the tailstock for alignment and support.

8. Hollowing the interior in 1" increments.

9. Complete cutting the interior with the bowl gouge.

Using a bowl scraper

Many times the bowl gouge cannot complete the interior cuts near the bowl bottom center without lifting it from the bevel support. You will get an "unsupported cut" which is very difficult to control and may lead to catches! Here we could use a heavy-duty interior bowl scraper to complete the cut.

Scrapers should be held with the handle well above the cutting edge and the edge positioned at the centerline of the bowl *(Photo 10)*. Cuts are best done on the pull stroke, as they are less aggressive than pushing the scraper into the bowl.

Finishing the foot

- Remove the bowl from your chuck and prepare a jam chuck by turning a small piece of softwood round and adding a tenon. Insert the tenon into your chuck and tighten.
- True the edge and face of the piece, slightly coving in the face. This step is important every time the jam chuck is reused so that the bowl is well centered when placed on it.
- Place a piece of rubber, sandpaper or other protective material between the bowl and the jam chuck *(Photo 11)*, place the bowl over the jam chuck, and bring up the tailstock live center for support *(Photo 12)*. Tighten the tailstock into the initial spur drive hole remaining from the first step. This centers the bowl on the jam chuck.
- Turn away the majority of the tenon, shaping the bowl foot as you do so *(Photo 13)*. Retain a small portion of the tenon for support from the tailstock.
- Remove the completed bowl from the lathe and carve away the nub of wood from the tailstock support using a chisel or carving tool to cut away the remaining tenon. Sand the carved area and add finish. *(Photo 14)*

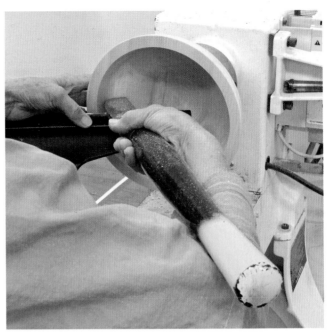

10. Use a bowl scraper to perfect the interior; be sure the cutting edge is trailing down to the center.

11. Set the bowl onto the jam chuck with a protecting pad.

12. To get the alignment, place the live center into the pinhole at the base of the tenon.

13. Reduce the tenon and complete the foot.

14. Your first bowl is completed.

6

Turning Your First Platter

Objectives

- Learn to use the four jaw scroll chuck with an expanding jaw hold.

- Learn to work with thin stock.

- Create more practice in transferring shapes and dimensions.

1. (above) These platters are made from 1" boards.

Supplies

- 9" x 9" x ¾" hardwood for your project (larger to fit your lathe if you wish).
- Yellow wood glue.
- Sandpaper and finish.
- Small hardwood plug to cover the live center point.
- 3" x 3" x 2" scrap wood and screws to attach to a faceplate to use as a glue block.
- Jam chuck from the last project.
- Deep fluted bowl gouge.
- Thickness calipers.
- Faceplate with glue block attached.
- Parting tool.
- Four jaw scroll chuck.

Discussion

Platters are both functional and simple to create. Think of them as just a shallow bowl. Particular attention needs to be given to the thickness measurements in order to avoid cutting through the project and creating a round picture frame. Since thinner stock is used, gluing it onto a faceplate/glue block assembly should start the project.

Starting on a glue block

A piece of cross grain hardwood is screwed to a faceplate as a project support technique that eliminates wasting precious project wood for making a tenon. This technique also allows the project to be removed from the lathe and reattached, retaining alignment that cannot be achieved by using a scroll chuck. When parting a project from a glue block, the block is wasted, not the project wood.

Making a glue block

When building a glue block, use a hardwood, not MDF or plywood. MDF and plywood are not stable or strong enough to hold larger projects and may delaminate. The wood should be cross grain so that the wood screws attaching to it will not pull out. Gluing your project to the cross grain wood will also be a stronger hold.

Using the four jaw scroll chuck with expanding jaws

In the past projects we have clamped the chuck jaw tightly *around* a tenon to hold the project. In this project we will *expand* the jaws into a groove made in the project bottom which is a different way of holding the project. Care must be taken using this technique to assure that there is enough wood outside the groove to not collapse when the jaws are opened into the groove. The jaws must set firmly on the flat base of the groove and not be opened with excessive force.

2. The blank is mounted onto a faceplate and glue block assembly and the corners removed.

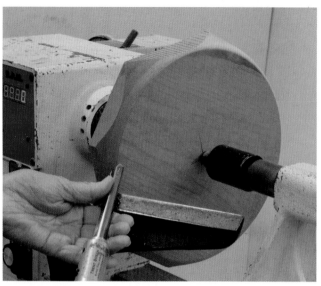

3. Round the edges of the blank from the face sides, maintaining the rule of 45's.

4. Flatten the face by using pull cuts, with the flute facing the turner at 45 degrees.

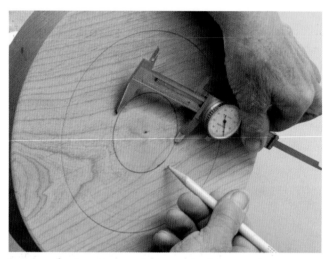

5. Lay out the platter rim area and tenon diameter.

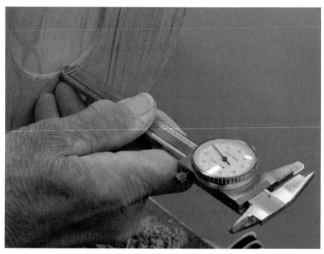

6. Be sure to have an exact depth measurement of the recess for the expanding jaws.

Activity

- Prepare to mount your platter blank by making the glue block assembly and mounting it on the lathe. True up the edges and flatten the face dead flat and ready to glue on the platter blank.
- Cut the platter blank from ¾" thick stock, marking the center on both sides. Remove the corners on a band saw.
- Glue the best face side of the blank to the glue block with yellow wood glue, using the tailstock for alignment and pressure (Photo 2). The glue should dry for at least two hours.

- Using a deep fluted gouge, carefully round the edges of the blank, cutting with the flute facing across the blank edge at 45 degrees (Photo 3). **You must cut from each edge toward the center to prevent major catches and torn grain. Take your time with this step!**
- Flatten the blank with a deep fluted gouge by making pull cuts facing the tool toward you and pulling it from the center toward the edge (Photo 4). Set the tool rest square across the face to guide the cuts.

7. The back side of the rim is shaped and sanded first.

8. Chuck the platter in the expanding jaws after removing the faceplate.

- Lay out your project *(Photo 5)* by marking the dimensions of the rim and the foot areas on the tail stock face of the blank. Remember that this is really the back of the platter. Mark your chuck recess diameter inside the foot area by closing the chuck's jaws, taking an outside measurement and transferring that dimension. Mark the thickness of the rim on the edge from the platter topside, the side glued to the glue block.
- Cut the recess to fit your chuck's expanding jaws, being sure the recess is exactly ⅛" deep *(Photo 6)*. The edge of the recess must be shaped to match the expanding chuck jaws square, or slightly dovetailed if your chuck requires it. Complete the center by sanding it to completion. There will not be an opportunity to work in this area later.
- Shape the bottom of the rim by cutting with your bowl gouge from the center toward the rim in gentle sweeping cuts. This shapes the underside of the rim. Sand and complete this area from rim to the area marked for the foot. *(Photo 7)*

9. Layout the platter rim on the face to align with the backside.

- Unscrew the faceplate from the glue block and reverse the platter into the recess previously cut for the chuck jaws *(Photo 8)*. Remember to not overtighten the jaws. Turn away the glue block carefully and reposition the tailstock to support the platter center.
- After re-flattening the platter face, layout the top of the rim area to align with the bottom turned portion *(Photo 9)*. Use a pulling cut from the center toward the edge to protect the slim platter edge.

10. Shape the interior of the rim and slightly start to cut the bowl.

11. Shape the bowl area carefully, retaining the center for depth measurement.

12. Complete the interior by removing any remaining ridges and sanding.

13. Set up the jam chuck to hold the platter without marring the completed center.

- Turn the rim area by reducing the thickness and matching the bottom curve with your bowl gouge. Begin to shape the bowl area to define the inside edge of the rim. Sand and complete the rim.
- Shape the interior bowl area *(Photos 10 and 11)* watching the thickness carefully. The exact center area can be left until the very end and used to measure the depth that has been turned away. In measuring the thickness, remember to subtract the chuck recess depth from your measurement (⅛").

- Complete the platter interior *(Photo 12)* by finally removing the center area, completing the shaping and removing any remaining ridges. Finally sand the interior.
- Remove the platter from the chuck. Place a jam chuck with rubber pad in your scroll chuck. *(Photo 13)*
- Add a small wood block over the point of the live center to protect the platter's completed foot area *(Photo 14)*. Adjust the platter's position to center it perfectly and tighten the tailstock for support.

14. Support the base with a protector on the live center point.

15. Remove additional wood from between the foot and the center and sand.

16. Here is the final project complete.

- Remove excess stock from the base, sand, and add a finish. *(Photos 15 and 16)*
- An alternate completion method requires the purchase of a set of "jumbo jaws" appropriate for your chuck. These jaws replace the chuck's standard jaws and grab the platter by the rim, giving full access to the center section for completion. If you choose to purchase and use large jaws, do not set the lathe speed to more than 1000 RPM.

Working with Green Wood

Objectives

- Learn how to harvest and prepare green wood for bowl turning.

- Learn the additional steps necessary for dealing with wood movement and green wood bowl drying.

1. (above) Green bowl blanks, roughed out and drying.

Discussion

One of the best sources of wood for turning bowls is the "urban forest." Trees cut in our neighborhoods and properly processed are constant sources of turning stock. Tree trimmers and arborists do not generally cut trees into pieces suitable for wood turners, so it is helpful for you to be present when the tree is cut down or trimmed. Many local hardwood species can be perfect bowl blanks, whereas most non-deciduous varieties are not so good. It is an interesting challenge for the new turner to learn which local species work the best.

The following illustrations depict the steps in cutting bowl blanks and storing them until you are ready to turn. Quick handling is most important in the warmer months when the wood dries rapidly. If the wood is not processed with speed, the drying will cause the wood to split and render it unusable.

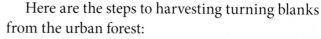

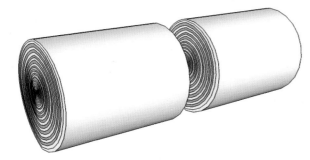

2. Cut logs 20% longer than their diameter.

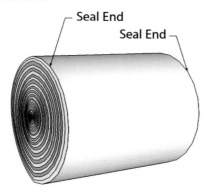

— Seal End

Seal End —

3. If you don't process the logs immediately, seal the ends.

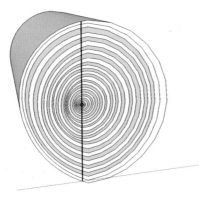

4. Find the symmetry through the log's pith.

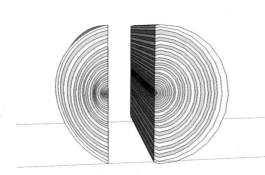

5. Cut along the symmetry line on both sides of the pith.

Here are the steps to harvesting turning blanks from the urban forest:

- Cut the tree into log sections approximately 20% longer than the tree is in diameter, thus allowing for some checking on the ends before the wood is completely processed. *(Drawing 2)*
- Seal the ends of each log section with a wax solution if the wood will not be processed immediately. Other end grain sealing agents also will work, such as inexpensive or surplus latex house paint (your color choice). *(Drawing 3)*
- To prepare and store the bowl blanks created from the log sections, stand the log section on end and locate the pith of the log (the center of growth). Rotate a straight edge around the pith, examining the log to locate two portions that appear to be as symmetrical as possible, and mark a line along that axis. *(Drawing 4)*
- Cut the log into two portions along the marked line bypassing the pith on both sides. The pith of the tree is unstable or dead wood and must be excluded from the bowl blanks to keep them from splitting. *(Drawing 5)*
- Reseal the ends with a wax solution or latex paint to prevent rapid moisture loss from the bowl blanks. Store the cut bowl blanks in a cool, airy location until they are rough turned. Allow for air circulation to prevent mold accumulation on or in the bowl blanks. *(Drawing 6)*

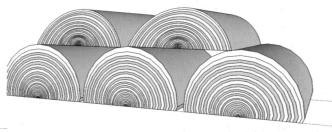

6. Store the prepped blanks in a cool, airy location.

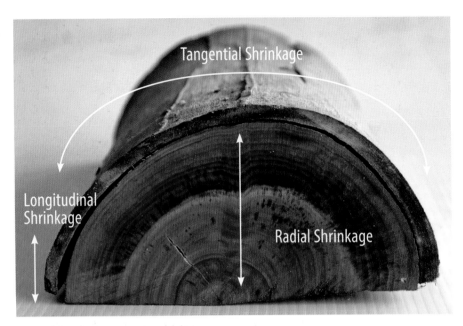

7. Wood moves in three directions as it dries.

Wood Movement

All species of wood shrink as they dry. As the cellular structures lose water, the cells shrink. Because shrinkage is not equal in all directions, drying wood distorts. The image above shows the relationship between the three directions of movement, and the table below lists the degree to which several well-known species move.

When turning green wood, woodturners must note this movement and plan for it. Turning green wood therefore is a multiple step process: rough turning, allowing the rough bowl to dry and shrink, and re-turning to bring the form back and complete the project.

Wood species	% Radial shrinkage	% Tangential shrinkage
Domestic hardwoods		
Ash, White	4.9	7.8
Poplar	3.0	7.1
Elm, American	4.2	9.5
California Laurel	3.0	9.0
Madrone, Pacific	5.6	12.4
Maple, Silver	3.9	7.2
Mesquite	2.2	2.6
Oak, Live	6.6	9.5
Tanoak	4.9	11.7
Walnut, Black	5.5	7.8
Domestic softwoods		
Cedar, Western Red	2.4	5.0
Douglas Fir, Coastal	4.8	7.6
Pine, Western White	4.1	7.4
Redwood, Young growth	2.2	4.9
Imports		
Bubinga	5.8	8.4
Cocobolo	3.0	4.0
Purple Heart	3.2	6.1
Rosewood, Brazilian	2.9	4.6

8. Rough out the bowl blanks to a wall thickness of about 10% of the diameter.

First step: Rough turning green wood bowl blanks

Green wood blanks are heavier due to the water content and more prone to shaking the lathe. Keep the lathe speed to its lowest setting until you know that the blank has been turned sufficiently to bring it into better balance. You will spend a large portion of the roughing out process in just getting the blank balanced and round. *(Photo 8)*

Safety at all times requires the turner to wear a full face shield during this phase, as there is always the possibility of flying bark or wood coming off the lathe.

- For a standard finished edge bowl, mount the green blank with the bark toward the tailstock. Cut away the bark where the live center is to be fitted in order to have a better hold on solid wood.

- The water and sap from green blanks will easily rust your lathe, so take precautions by waxing the ways, tool rest, and banjo. Also clean up soon after completing the roughing out process.

- Roughing out is the process of initially turning the green blank into its general shape before allowing it to dry. The bowl blank can be mounted on a screw chuck, as we did in the last exercise for initial turning, or between centers using a spur drive in the headstock.

If you mount between centers, recheck the tightness regularly as the fibers compress and the hold loosens over time.

- When adding the tenon before roughing out the interior, be sure that the tenon is in solid wood with no bark, since bark won't hold. Also make the tenon larger than initially needed as it will be reduced later when the bowl is turned the second time.

- Hollow the interior, allowing for a wall thickness of 10% of the total diameter or 1" thickness. This is necessary to allow for the distortion during the drying phase that will naturally occur. The wall thickness must be uniform from top to bottom. Uneven wall thickness will allow drying in the thinner areas more rapidly than in the thicker areas causing added strain and potential cracking.

Second step: Sealing, storing & drying

- The roughed out blank is sealed on all surfaces with a wax solution, latex house paint, or any material that will reduce the rate of drying. Most important is to seal the end grain areas inside and outside, as moisture will be more rapidly lost through these areas.

- Roughed out blanks should be stored in a cool location with good air circulation so that the drying can proceed slowly and evenly *(Photo 9)*. Weighing the blank and noting its weight

9. Seal and store rough bowl blanks until dry.

periodically can check the drying process. When the weight loss stops, the blank will be nearing dryness. A purchased moisture meter will be more accurate.

- Many wood turners will place the roughed out bowl in a kraft paper bag with chips from the initial turning. The paper slows down the moisture loss rate and reduces the probability of cracking due to rapid shrinking. (*Photo 10*)

- It is also a good idea to mark the date, wood species, etc., on the base of the tenon, as you may not recall this information later.

Third step: Remounting and re-turning
After the blank is dry (maybe three to six months–possibly longer), it is remounted and re-turned.

- Mount the blank between a jam chuck (tenon facing the tailstock) and a live center in order to re-true the tenon before placing it in the scroll chuck. (This is why you made the tenon oversized earlier.) While in this orientation, some of the exterior of the rough turned blank can be re-turned to correct for the drying distortion.

- Now reverse the bowl blank into the four jaw scroll chuck and continue to reshape the exterior until the project is back in relative

10. Blanks distort more in the direction of the growth rings as they dry.

balance. This will allow you to increase the lathe speed in the next step for better interior cuts. If you are working on the bowl's exterior after re-chucking, the cuts will be from the headstock toward the tailstock in order to cut downhill and get the cleanest cuts.

- Clean up the interior and reduce the wall thickness in 1" increments to the desired final design.

- Use a jam chuck or jumbo jaws to complete the foot, as described earlier for the dry wood bowl project.

Turning a Natural Edge Bowl

Objectives

- Learn how natural edge bowls differ from finished edge bowls in the turning process.

- Learn techniques for adjusting and aligning the blank.

- Experience turning "air" as part of the process.

1. (above) Natural edge bowls have the bark edge at the top.

Discussion

How natural edge bowls differ

When turning a natural edge bowl, the resulting bowl will be substantially smaller than a comparable finished edge bowl from the same blank.

There will be many cuts where the woodturner will be cutting air—wood—air—wood, etc. Therefore the tools must be correctly anchored to the body and tool rest and not allowed to climb into the openings offered. It is helpful to increase the turning speed as soon as possible so the tool has fewer tendencies to slip into the voids.

Activity

Working with the half-log

- In turning natural edged bowls, the blank is mounted with the outer surface (bark side) mounted toward the headstock and the flat inner wood surface mounted toward the tailstock. This is the reversed orientation to the finished edge bowl of the last chapter. Be sure to remove a large area of bark where the spur drive will be placed to allow the spur to bite into hard wood for a safer hold. (*Photo 2*)

  Mounting the blank between centers with a spur drive and live center allows for some readjustment that may be required during the turning process to get the wings of the bowl even and level with each other. Most designs require the lower wings and the high wings to be aligned with each other. In order to accomplish this, the position of the live center may need to be moved up/down or left/right as the turning proceeds. (*Photo 3*)

- As we begin to make the bowl shape, we reach the first bark area—the lower wings. Turn the lathe off and rotate the project by hand to measure whether the wings are of similar height.

  If they are not, then the position of the live center in the tail stock is moved one half of the distance of the misalignment to bring them into better alignment (*Photo 4*). The outside will again be out of alignment and will be recut to bring the blank back into balance.

  Don't forget to cut the tenon for use in the next step.

  Finally, the turning proceeds and the rim of the bowl is reached. The high wings are also measured in the same manner and a readjustment in the live center may again be needed.

  When the exterior is completed (*Photo 5*), the bowl should be sanded and then reversed into the scroll chuck. We won't be able to easily cut this area later.

2. Drill out the bark to give the live center a solid bite into the hard wood.

3. Check the balance between the wings to assure symmetry.

4. You may need to adjust the blank alignment to get the wings balanced.

5. Completing the exterior reveals the balanced upper and lower wings.

- Start turning away the wood on the interior using the same three-phase cut as before. As the interior is reduced, the high bark edges and the upper wings will become fragile, unsupported, and subject to vibration. Therefore completing the bowl from the rim to the bottom must be done in steps. As the cuts deepen into the bowl, there is less and less support, and movement at the rim increases. You can't go back to the rim later as it will be unstable and subject to catches or possibly total project destruction.

  Turn the interior to just below the lowest bark wing area into the solid wood and to about 1" wall thickness (*Photo 6*). Keep the center of the blank solid for maximum support and minimum vibration.

- Complete the first inch to final wall thickness (*Photo 7*) by increasing your lathe speed if possible, and recutting the first 1" to the final

6. Start to cut the interior down to solid wood.

7. Complete the first inch to final wall thickness.

8. Complete the second inch, blending it into the first portion.

9. Continue cutting 1" at a time all the way to the bottom.

10. Here is the finished bowl with balanced wings.

wall thickness. Check the uniformity of the wall regularly with your calipers.

Because you are cutting both air and wood alternatively, be sure the bowl gouge flute is vertical to the bowl's edge and the bevel parallel with the outside wall face. This will reduce the possibility of the tool skating off and tearing the edge.

- Now finalize another inch in the same manner (*Photo 8*), repeating the same cuts for another inch of depth. After completing the second inch of depth, carefully blend it into the earlier first inch with very light cuts or with your interior bowl scraper. Continue these steps one inch at a time until the bowl gouge can no longer maintain a bevel-rubbing cut against the interior wall.

- When the bottom of the bowl is reached (*Photo 9*) or the bowl gouge can no longer maintain a bevel-rubbing cut, switch to using the heavy duty bowl scraper to round the inside shape of the bottom. As the bowl deepens it may be useful to rotate the tool rest into the bowl to bring the cutting edge closer to the surface being worked. When you move the tool rest, always recheck clearances by manually rotating the bowl before turning the lathe on.

- To complete the bowl's foot, use a jam chuck, as in the previous projects. Since there may be deep wings, it may be necessary to make a new jam chuck that is taller than the one previously used. (*Photo 10*)

1. Goblets are turned both end grain and side grain.

End Grain Turning

Objectives

- Learn end grain hollowing techniques.
- Learn to drill with a shallow fluted gouge.

Supplies

- Wood blank 3" x 3" x 8".
- Four jaw chuck.
- Spindle roughing gouge (SRG).
- Shallow fluted gouge.
- Parting tool and calipers.
- Sandpaper and finish.
- Tennis ball (well used).

Discussion

Turning a goblet introduces the new turner to a third turning orientation, turning end grain, which requires cutting into the end of the wood fibers with an edge tool or a scraper. Goblet turning is a combination of turning a spindle and turning a small end grain bowl. This project can be repeated with a green tree branch of increasing length as an additional fun exercise. The goblet is a nice introduction to turning end grain and an opportunity to improve your spindle turning skills as well.

We will also continue to work with end grain in the next chapter.

Remember, "downhill to the grain"? In spindle turning it is toward the center of the spindle; in bowl turning it is base to rim outside and rim to bottom inside. In end grain turning it is from the center of the wood outward. To work from the center outward, it is easier to drill a pilot hole large enough to insert the shallow fluted gouge. This can be done with standard drill bits or with a shallow fluted gouge, as in this example.

Since most goblets have slim stems that will not support turning work on the cup area, the turning must be completed from the top of the goblet toward the base. The longer the stem or the thinner it is the more difficult the project becomes.

Activity

- Prepare the stock by mounting between centers, turning it round and adding a tenon for your scroll chuck. Remount the blank in your four jaw scroll chuck and bring up the tailstock for additional support. Re-true the blank if it is necessary.
- Shape the exterior of the cup portion (*Photo 2*) with a shallow fluted gouge at the tailstock end of the project wood. Do not reduce the stem diameter at this time. We need it for support until after the interior of the cup is hollowed out. Remove the tailstock from the lathe.

2. Begin by shaping the cup exterior.

3. You are ready to drill with the shallow fluted gouge exactly at the center line.

- Drill a hole into the end (*Photo 3*). You can use a Jacob's chuck and drill bit or drill with a shallow fluted gouge. Try using the shallow fluted gouge technique by adjusting your tool rest to set the cutting edge of the gouge to be exactly at the center of the blank.

  Note that you cannot use a bowl gouge for this operation, as the shape will not cut properly.

- With the lathe running at a moderate speed, approximately 1200 RPM, press the gouge straight into the center, keeping the handle level. Remove waste and reintroduce the gouge

4. Drill a depth hole to about 90% of the cup's depth.

5. Measure the depth of the cup with the gouge.

6. Position the gouge at 45 degrees to hollow out the cup. Hollow by pushing the handle backward and pivoting around the left thumb.

several times until you reach approximately 90% of the cup depth. (*Photo 4*)

- You can also use the gouge to check the depth of the hole. (*Photo 5*)
- Shape the inside of the cup (*Photo 6*) by opening the interior from the center outward, with the gouge held at approximately 45-degrees counter clockwise to rotation. Before starting, increase the lathe speed to approximately 1800 RPM, as you will be working at the center where wood moves past the cutting edge at a lower inches-per-minute surface speed. (The smaller the diameter, the

less surface speed past the cutting edge for any given RPM.)

- Hold the rotated tool in your right hand, pinch the shaft at the tool rest with the left hand, and cut by moving the right hand horizontally away from the lathe to the rear. To go deeper, slowly advance the tool, remembering to swing the handle backward for each cut. Focus on keeping the tool at the 45-degree orientation; too vertical and it will catch, too and horizontal it will cut poorly.
- Check the wall thickness and depth frequently with your fingers or a set of calipers.

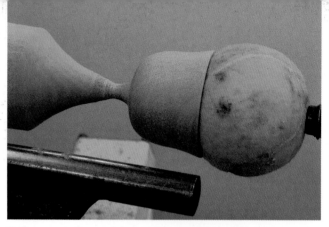

7. Support the goblet with a tennis ball.

8. After completing the stem, undercut the base.

9. Part off with a smooth cut to reduce the amount of sanding.

- Complete the cup interior by sanding through all the desired grits, as you will not be able to work in this area later. Measure the exact depth turned and transfer that measurement to the exterior of the blank for use in the next step.
- Replace the tailstock and insert a tennis ball into the completed goblet cup and hold it in place with the tailstock live center for support (*Photo 7*). Turn the exterior of the cup, observing the marked depth. Turn the stem by reducing it carefully from the tailstock end toward the headstock, still using the shallow fluted gouge.
- Shape the base last (*Photo 8*). Its size is generally about the same diameter or slightly larger than the cup portion. When completed, sand the exterior.
- Part off the goblet (*Photo 9*) by using your parting tool with several overlapping cuts to prevent binding. As you cut, angle the

10. Here is the completed project.

tool slightly toward the tailstock. This will undercut the base and allow the goblet to stand level. As you complete the cuts toward the center, you may choose to turn off the lathe and complete the parting off with a small saw.

The bottom of the base will have to be sanded and finished by hand, so it is a good idea to make as clean a parting cut as you can to reduce the later work. (*Photo 10*)

End Grain Boxes — Making Things Fit

10

Objectives

- Learn to turn carefully to make parts fit perfectly.
- Make and use custom fitting jam chucks.

1. (above) Small boxes from scrap hardwoods are carefully cut from end grain.

Supplies

- Straight grain hardwood 3" x 3' x 6".
- SRG.
- Shallow fluted gouge.
- Parting tools ¼" and a narrow ¹⁄₁₆".
- ½" round nose box scraper.
- Vernier calipers to transfer dimensions.

Discussion

Small boxes are a passion for some turners as they make great gifts and display your favorite woods beautifully. There are two major challenges: performing the turning

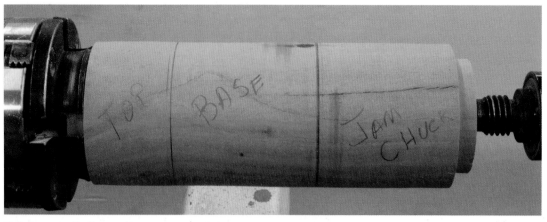

2. Lay out all dimensions.

3. Add the base tenon, then make a thin parting cut near the lid.

4. Part off the base and its tenon, leaving a small tenon for reference.

steps in the correct order and making the parts fit correctly. Approach fitting your components by carefully testing the fit, cutting a little more, and retesting. Speed is not your friend.

Since the lid and the box both are worked inside and outside, they must be completed in the exact order proposed or the project may not be completed at all. Watch the steps carefully and you will be successful.

As in the goblet project, there will be end grain hollowing with the shallow fluted gouge and probably a small round nosed box scraper. The scraper is added to improve the quality of the interior cuts and reduce the amount of sanding necessary. Also, most boxes are deeper than the cup portion of the goblet and may be difficult to complete with a gouge.

Activity

- Prepare the stock by mounting the blank between centers and rounding out. Add a tenon on both ends. Mark out your box by penciling in lines at ¼, ½, ¼, and labeling each section as is illustrated. (*Photo 2*)
- Place the lid tenon (top end) in your four jaw chuck. With your parting tool, add a shallow parting cut about ³⁄₁₆"deep and about the same width at the line separating the lid from the box. This will be used to fit the lid/base together. (*Photo 3*)
- Part off the base/jam chuck section from the lid with a narrow parting tool, leaving only a small portion of the parting cut on the lid side for dimensional reference (*Photo 4*). If you do not have a ¹⁄₁₆" parting tool, you may saw the

5. Drill out the depth of the lid and mark its depth.

6. Hollow out the lid with a gouge.

7. After cutting a square internal shoulder, test fit the base.

base off. The goal is to leave at least ¼" of the tenon remaining on the base. This will be needed to hold the lid.

- Using the shallow fluted gouge, shape the interior of the lid. It is helpful to drill a reference depth hole and mark that depth on the exterior of the lid. (*Photo 5*)
- Work from the center outward hollowing the lid carefully (*Photo 6*). You may also use a round nosed scraper to complete the final interior shaping. Use the small tenon stub as a reference while hollowing to be sure not to go beyond that dimension.

- Square the inside of the lid, removing the remaining tenon stub carefully (*Photo 7*). The goal is to create a groove inside the lid to fit tightly onto the tenon remaining on the box body section. As you use a parting tool to carefully create the groove in small steps, keep the inside shoulder of the lid edge absolutely square by holding the tool parallel with the ways of the lathe. Test fit the base onto the new square shoulder until it fits tightly.

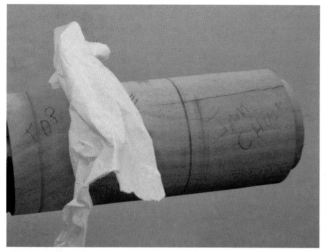

8. If the lid is too a loose, use a paper shim.

9. Mount the base in the chuck, attach the lid and shape the exterior.

10. Complete the top of the lid carefully, pushing toward the base only.

11. Hollow the box with a gouge or a round nosed scraper.

- Sand and finish the inside of the lid, being careful not to change the inside of the lid shoulder. The inside of the lid is done and will not be reworked later.

  Sometimes accidents or impatience happen and the fit is loose and unable to be supported when turning the exterior. In this case, gasket material can be added to tighten the fit. Try facial tissue or paper towels to get the fit very tight (*Photo 8*). This fit will be loosened later after the lid's exterior is finished.

- Mount the base section in the four jaw chuck using the end tenon initially created.

Firmly attach the lid to the base. Bring up the tailstock for additional support (*Photo 9*).

Shape the exterior of the box and lid, blending the two together into a smooth shape.

- Remove the tailstock and carefully complete the top of the lid. Refer to your pencil marking for the interior depth and be careful not to cut into the lid interior! (*Photo 10*)

- Make the final cuts on the lid very carefully and don't press across the top of the lid with heavy pressure; avoid dislodging the lid from the box. The lid is now complete and can be put aside while the base is developed.

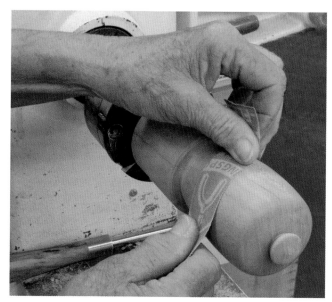

12. Sand and complete the exterior.

13. Part the base from the remaining jam chuck material.

- Using your shallow fluted gouge, drill a depth hole into the box and mark the final depth onto the exterior of the base section with your pencil (*Photo 11*). Hollow the base in the same fashion as you did the lid interior, stopping the cut at least ³⁄₁₆" from the inside of the tenon so it does not become too weak. A round nosed scraper can be used to smoothly complete the shaping of the interior.
- Sand and complete the interior of the base. After the hollowing of the box, re-test the lid fit. It may now be looser and more acceptable for the finished product. If it is still too tight for use, lightly sand the tenon to reduce the tight fit.
- Recheck the depth on the exterior in preparation for parting off the base. Make a parting cut approximately 30%-40% of the needed depth at the bottom of the box. Complete the shaping of the box's base section. Sand and complete the finishing of the base. Part off the base section from the jam chuck section. (*Photos 12 and 13*)
- Carefully measure the outside diameter of the box tenon and transfer the measurement to the face of the flattened and smoothed jam chuck still remaining in the scroll chuck.

14. Make the final jam chuck to fit the box body.

- Using a parting tool or square nosed scraper, turn away the *inside* of the mark (*Photo 14*), test fitting the base onto the jam chuck for a tight fit. This will allow you to turn the bottom of the box. Remember that the cuts must be straight and square for the box to fit tightly.

- Turn the bottom of the box base (*Photo 15*), slightly undercutting it. Work carefully, pressing toward the headstock while making the cuts. Sand and finish the bottom. (*Photo 16*)
- Attach the lid and you are done. (*Photo 17*)

15. Complete the bottom of the box.

16. Add a coat of finish to complete.

17. Here is the finished box.

11

Completing Your Projects

Objectives

- Learn more about sanding your projects.
- Learn some useful finishing techniques.

Discussion

The sanding process

Sanding is the process of scratching the wood surface with finer and finer scratches until the abrasions are invisible. After all the work and effort in creating the project, it is important to make it as presentable and fit for its intended use as possible. The work of creation does not end with the turning. To make your work as complete as desired may require more time than the actual turning did! Here are a few guidelines to help.

- Use the best sandpaper you can buy and discard it when it begins to wear. This will save you a *lot* of time by always using sharp paper that cuts correctly. Worn 80-grit paper does not become 120-grit—only 80-grit that won't cut any more.
- Always follow the order of grits: 80, 120, 180, 220, and 320. Don't skip grits in a rush or earlier scratches may not be completely removed.
- After sanding with the lathe running, turn off the lathe and hand sand in the direction of the grain to remove all circular scratches caused in the previous sanding step. You can remove a lot of stubborn scratches this way.
- Keep the lathe speed low as high speed sanding generates surface heat and can cause small surface cracks to appear.
- Don't proceed to the next grit until all circular marks are gone. It may require a bright light to see the marks clearly.

- If scratches reappear as you work in finer grits, they were always there and are only now being seen due to the smoother surface surrounding them. You must go back to the grit of sandpaper that created the scratches and rework the whole sanding process.
- Sanding wood and sanding a finished surface are different processes. There is no point in sanding a course-grained wood beyond 320-grit as the pores of the wood themselves may be larger than the grit of the sandpaper. Once finish is applied and the wood pores are filled, sanding between topcoats can proceed with even finer grits.

Sanding devices

In addition to hand sanding on the lathe, some mechanical accessories can speed the process and randomize the scratch patterns at the same time.

Inertial sanders (*Photo 1*) are devices that freely rotate as the wood turns on the lathe. The edge of the device is rested against the wood as the lathe rotates, causing the sander to counter rotate. This reverse rotation creates a more random sanding pattern and can vastly speed up the transition between grits.

Because these devices use Velcro™ and Velcro™ backed sanding disks, pressing too hard causes increased sanding heat and the plastic Velcro™ "hook and loops" can melt and cause the device to fail. Keep it cool.

Power sanders (*Photo 2*) also rotate the paper on Velcro™ or PSA (pressure sensitive adhesive) pads held in the jaws of a power drill. This is very useful, and can also speed the sanding process since the lathe does not need to be turning to create sanding action. This allows more aggressive sanding to be done. Additionally, they can be used to spot sand areas of projects that cannot be sanded with the lathe operating, such as areas with voids and irregular surfaces or the wings on a natural edged bowl.

Dust collectors (*Photo 3*) are also a needed sanding "tool", as dust should be removed from

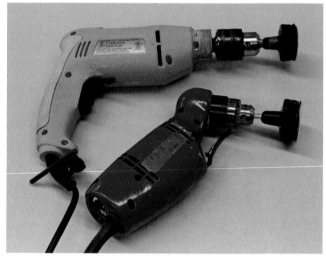

1. Inertial sanders operate with the lathe's rotating motion.

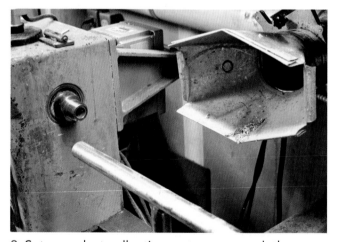

2. Power drills with sanding disks attached can be more aggressive.

3. Set up a dust collection system at your lathe.

the immediate area for the lathe operator's health. Latent dust in the finishing area will also affect the finishing steps later. Even a small portable dust collector installed behind your lathe will aid in collecting sanding dust.

Since collectors can't get all the dust, you should always remember to wear a dust mask of high quality to protect yourself. We recommend masks that are marked to meet the NIOSH N-95 standard.

Finishing

There are two classes of finishes;:those that penetrate into the wood structure and build from the bottom up and film coatings that seal the surface and add additional layers of protection.

Penetrating finishes include linseed oil, tung oil, polymerized oils, and oil/varnish blends. Film coatings include reactive varnishes, shellac, lacquer and wax.

- Wax *(Photo 4)* adds a quick shine, makes the wood feel slick under the hand and provides some abrasive protection. Wax does not wear well and is generally reserved for "topping off" as a final coat over other finishes. By itself wax should be reserved for decorative projects only—things that will not be routinely used or handled.

- Only a few oils applied to wood surfaces will totally dry (oxidize). Oils penetrate into the wood, enhance the appearance of the grain and provide some amount of protection for the surface. Over time they will wear away and will need to be renewed. Without chemical drying agents they may require several days to totally dry. More likely to be used are oils modified with chemical drying agents such as "boiled" linseed oil, polymerized Tung oil, or Tru-Oil. Most oils are food safe and digestible when totally dry and all the smells have left, indicating that no more chemical evaporation is occurring. Be aware also of the possibility of nut oil allergies in some individuals.

4. Typical paste waxes are available from hardware stores and woodworking dealers.

5. Only a few penetrating oils will totally dry.

Be aware that some oils such as cooking oils from the grocery store do not fully dry, remain "tacky" and can become rancid over time.

- Varnishes such as Minwax™ Poly, Waterlox™, Watco™, Verathane™, and GF Salad Bowl Finish™ are more resistant to heat, water and wear and are a more frequently applied turning finish *(Photo 6)*. Surfaces from matte to high gloss can be achieved with the application of multiple coats built up over time. Varnishes contain a blend of several

6. The most widely used finishes are the urethane oil varnishes.

components, including drying oils, urethane co-polymers, and volatile organic carriers. Each brand contains a proprietary blend of these components. The nut oils penetrate and dry by oxidation, the urethane molecules polymerize into polyurethane and the VOC's (volatile organic compounds) evaporate leaving a food safe surface. While these surfaces may be wiped with a damp cloth they are not dishwasher safe. Most "urethane oils" (varnishes) will act as their own sealer coat.

- Shellac is a film coating used in many cases as a first coat sealer because it dries quickly, adds little color and bonds easily to most other finishes. Shellac itself is a relatively poor topcoat since it has poor resistance to water, heat, chemicals and wear. Shellac is the product of the Lac beetle dissolved in alcohol, and is also a food safe coating. Shellac has a shelf life of a few months. When old it does not dry well, or at all. When using shellac as a sealer, use only de-waxed, super blond as it will not add additional color to the wood.

- Sprayed or brushed lacquers are quick to apply and dry by evaporation of the solvents. Additional coats can be applied while earlier coats are still wet. The later coats dissolve into the earlier coats, forming a single continuous surface. There is no limit to the thickness that can be built up. While coats can quickly be

applied, the result is only moderately resistant to heat, water and wear. Also be aware that the evaporative vapors are very flammable and toxic. There is a long learning curve for properly applying lacquers effectively.

If you want a glass-like surface, sand between each coat with 220-grit papers to remove most of the surface coating down to the wood pores and reapply the finish. Repeat this process until the pores are completely filled with finish "filling the pot holes." Later coats of finish can now be added and leveled out with 0000 steel wool and buffed to a final gloss.

Always build coats with "gloss"-labeled varnishes, as "matte" and "semi-gloss" finishes contain optical diffraction agents to scatter the light; building coats with these will create a surface that has little depth and may appear cloudy. If you desire a matte or semi-gloss final finish, rough up the top coat with 0000 steel wool or use a matte finish for the final top coat only.

Troubleshooting Your Projects

Gouges, catches, and digs

A catch is a sudden deepening of the cut due to the positioning of the cutting tool in such a manner that more wood is suddenly presented to the cutting edge. Generally this happens when the tool is turned in too aggressive a position or the tool's bevel ceases to support the cutting action.

After such a catch, the lathe should be turned off and the tool placed into the damaged area to find an angle or rotation where the tool just fits. Then you can easily determine where the tool was during the dramatic surprise and correct that action in future cuts.

In spindle turning, minimize catches by first rubbing the bevel, then advancing the tool into the cut by raising the handle in the direction of the tool's flute. Remember, when cutting a bead or cove the tool's flute will not always be pointing vertically.

Also determine that the cut is always happening on the lower side of the tool. If the tool is rotated too far and the upper edge engages, there is a high probability that this will lead to an eventual catch and torn grain.

When turning the interior of a bowl, many catches occur when the curving sidewall of the bowl transitions sharply into the curve across the bottom. As the tool moves toward the bottom and the handle is not rotated quickly enough, the cut suddenly moves to the tip and the wrong side of the tool, which is very open. The gouge suddenly grabs too much wood.

Catches also happen with bowl scrapers when the handle is not raised higher than the scraping edge of the tool. Again, too much wood is grabbed. To minimize this, rest the tool on top of the right forearm, raising the tool rest to a position where the cutting edge is at the centerline of the bowl *(Photo 7)*. Moving the arm and body around the intended curve accomplishes the cutting.

Making the cut from the bottom of the bowl upward toward the rim, a pull cut can ease the cut of the scraper. This reduces the pressure of the tool tip against the wood and lightens the cut.

Torn grain

Torn grain occurs when the unsupported fibers of the wood are lifted away from the surface and ripped off or pulled out. You can usually see this effect on the exterior of a cross-grain bowl at the end grain area. The trailing edge of the end grain cuts well and the leading edge does not since the fibers are unsupported. *(Drawings 8 and 9)*

There are many causes of torn grain: dull tools, pushing the tool too hard or too fast, turning at a lathe speed that is too slow, the tendency of some soft-fiber wood to easily fray, and just bad luck.

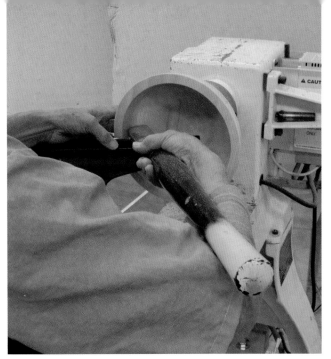

7. Support the scrapers on top of your arm to assure the safest cutting angle.

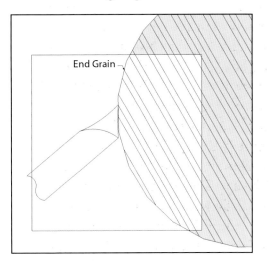

8. The trailing edge of the end grain with supported fibers being cut.

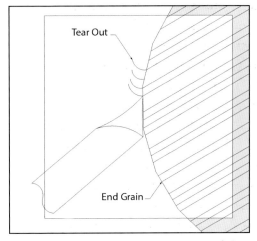

9. The unsupported leading edge of the end grain leads to potential tear out.

A Lesson Plan for Woodturning | 77

Addressing torn grain issues

Sanding is not a solution to torn grain; recutting the torn grain area with adjustments must be done.

- Resharpen your tool and take a lighter cut with a faster lathe speed.
- Use a smaller diameter gouge to bring the cutting edge closer to the supporting bevel.
- Change the tool geometry to allow the bevel to move closer to the cutting edge providing more support to the cut. Try shortening the bevel length by grinding some of the heel away.
- Stiffen the fibers to hold them in place while the tool cuts by applying a coat of shellac before the final cut.
- If possible, reverse the lathe direction and recut with the opposite rotation. This may or may not help, as now the grain in the opposite direction is a risk!

Splits and cracks

Cracks, splits or broken out inclusions may mar your work. Splits and cracks should be attended to immediately to prevent accidents and the worsening of the fault. On smaller cracks, use super glue (thin) poured carefully into the crack with some matching sawdust added. The glue will discolor the surface of the wood, especially light colored woods; but in many cases the finish applied at the end will hide the discoloration. Be sure the glue has set before turning the lathe back on.

Larger cracks, inclusions or voids can be filled with epoxy mixed with filler that blends or contrasts with the project. Using epoxy will allow for the wood movement, as epoxy is flexible and will expand and contract with the wood.

Really large cracks are good reasons to discard the wood totally. Don't spend time working with a project that has a high probability of failure and may be dangerous.

12

Where to Go Next

As you progress to a greater skill level, you should become more critical of your output by trying to determine what you could do differently, if you were to repeat that same project.

Make an idea book to keep a collection of pictures of objects you have seen and would like to try. Collect them into sections of similar projects for easier review. Trying out new ideas or more challenging techniques are ways to develop more skills and knowledge.

When you undertake a new project, have an approach and a drawing of what you intend to do. If you are selecting an expensive piece of wood for this project, consider making a prototype first with a less expensive species. This way you can work out any unforeseen problems without sacrificing the "good stuff."

Joining an organization such as the local chapter of the American Association of Woodturners or a local woodworking club gives you exposure to new ideas, opportunity for critique, and the camaraderie you need in your new craft.

There are also many web sites, discussion groups, and on-line membership groups that can add to your knowledge base.

However, there is nothing like getting into the shop and making something! The more you use your tools and lathe, the more your muscles will develop memory for the motions needed. As a caution, remember:

- Always wear safety glasses.
- Don't work when you are tired.
- Don't rush to finish.

Appendix I
Additional Projects

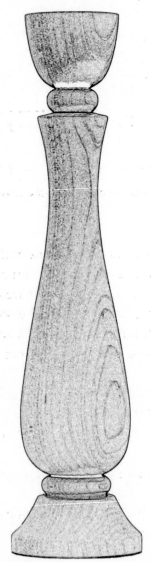

1. A candlestick is a more complex set of beads and coves matching a set of measurements.

Discussion

These additional projects allow more skill development, including making items to match a drawing, sizing projects to specific dimensions, and just trying fun stuff for the first time!

- **A candlestick** addresses transferring and reproducing dimensions from a plan and breaking the project into steps.
- **Turning a candlestick set** raises the ante by attempting to make multiples of the same object. This requires accurate layout, a "story stick," and careful, focused turning.
- **A three leg miniature stool** combines faceplate and spindle turning as well as duplication into one single project. Here you will also have to make a drilling fixture to get the leg angle correct.
- **A carver's mallet** is just fun and also is useful in the shop. Simple curves fitted to your hand.
- **Spin tops** are fun, fast and great gifts for kids. If you do the whole thing with your skew chisel you will become skilled very quickly!
- **Baseball bats** may look like more of the same but they are long and will be unstable and flexible in the center. This will require careful supported cuts.

Spindle Project— Candlestick or a Candlestick Set

Objectives
- Learn to turn more complex shapes.
- Learn to turn from drawings.
- Transfer dimensional drawing information to a project through direct measurement transfer and "story sticks."

Supplies
- One 3" x 3" x 9" hardwood blank for the first candlestick.
- One 3" x 3" x 9" blank for each additional candlestick.

Discussion
The difficulty of this project is in making three objects match. This requires more careful planning and transfer of the dimensions and diameters before starting to turn the shape. Making a set of three related candle sticks also requires some creative decisions concerning how to increase or reduce the dimension by 10%. To get the best results, don't skip making the drawings!

Activity
- Rough out a blank and transfer key transitions to its face. Transfer only the key dimensions. Be sure to start the project from the tailstock end of the wood.
- With your parting tool and a pair of calipers, transfer the key diameters at the pencil lines added above.
- Start turning the shapes from the tailstock end working toward the headstock end.

If you are making the set:
- Turn a second candlestick 10% smaller than the original by determining the new dimensions and creating an accurate scale drawing before starting.

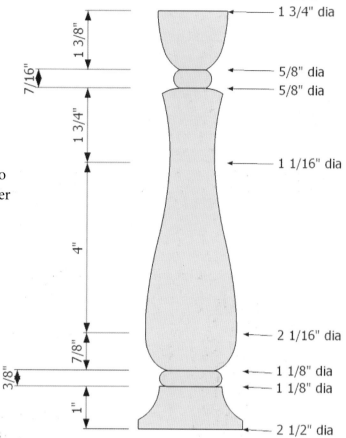

2. Here is a dimensional drawing for the candlestick.

- As with the first candlestick, transfer the dimensions and carefully turn it in the same manner. It will be important to assure that the shape pleasingly matches the first version.
- The third candlestick should be 10% larger than the original using the same processes.

Part One: Making the first candlestick
- Rough turn a blank between centers.
- Add a tenon and transfer the blank to a four-jaw chuck.
- Transfer dimensional information from the drawing.
- Turn the candlestick to match the drawing.
- Drill a candle taper recess in the top.
- Sand and part off.

Part Two: Designing and turning your own candlestick set

- Create a new drawing using a sheet of ¼" grid graph paper.
- Make this drawing similar to the original model except 10% smaller. Consider what proportions need to change and which need to remain the same. *(Photo 3)*
- Add appropriate dimensions to allow you to transfer the drawing to the lathe.
- Turn your designed candlestick in the same manner as above.
- Repeat the activity by making another new drawing, 10% larger than the original and repeating all the above steps.

3. Three candlesticks drawn to size at +/- 10% make a pleasant set.

Turn a Small Stool from a Given Drawing

Objectives

- Make the seat as a face plate project.
- Make three matching legs as spindle projects.
- Develop a "story stick" from the full scale drawing to assist in matching the legs.
- Produce the three stool legs exactly alike.

Supplies

- Stool seat blank 10" x 10" x 2" hardwood stock.
- Stool legs: three pieces of matching or contrasting hardwood 2" x 2" x 13".
- A ⅜" dowel cut to ¾" length used as a hole plug.
- Card stock or stiff paper to create full scale templates for turning the legs.

This project *(Photo 4)* requires both faceplate and spindle work. Matching the legs is the most challenging task. A fixture to drill the leg holes at a 15-degree splay will facilitate accurate drilling on a drill press. If you hand drill use two adjustable squares to line up the drill bit.

4. This small three-legged stool will fit any 10-inch lathe.

Activity

Part One: Turning a stool seat

Prepare the seat blank *(Photo 5)*
- Mark the dead center of the seat blank and draw a circle to allow the blank to fit on your lathe (9½" diameter for 10" lathes and 11" diameter for 12" lathes).
- At the band saw, trim the square blank to the pencil line.
- Using a drill press, drill a ⅜" hole 1" deep at the dead center location or other diameter as your chuck manufacturer requires.

Turn the seat profile *(See Drawing 10)*
- Using the screw chuck and your four-jaw chuck, screw on the seat blank, assuring that it sits completely flat against the chuck jaws.
- True the edge of the blank with the bowl gouge, approaching the edge from both faces.
- Square up the face of the seat blank first then "cup" the center of the seat blank to ¼" depth. Use a straight edge to check the curvature.
- Round over the top edge of the seat for comfort.
- Chamfer the bottom edge of the seat blank *(Photo 6)*, undercutting at about 45-degrees to improve the appearance of the seat's thickness.
- Sand the top and edges to final smoothness and remove the seat from the lathe.
- On the back side of the seat, mark a circle from the center to ½" from the chamfered bottom edge using a compass and a ⅜" peg glued into the center hole.
- Use the same compass setting to mark the penciled circle into six sections (do this action in both clock-wise and counter clock-wise directions). *(Photo 7)*
- Locate the center of every other set of markings and center punch an alignment mark. This is where you will drill the holes for the legs.
- Construct a straight line from the punched marks through the center point to the opposite

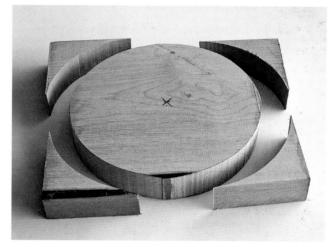

5. The seat blank ready to lathe mount.

6. Complete the seat profile by chamfering the back edge, ready to sand.

7. Laying out the alignment lines for drilling the leg holes.

side of the drawn circle. This will be used as a sight line to get the drilling straight.

- Create a drilling fixture to set a 15-degree leg splay angle, or set the table of your drill press at a 15-degree tilt. *(Photo 8)*
- Align each marked leg hole location in the drill press and drill a 1⅛" Forstner bit hole until all edges of the bit cut the wood, but no deeper. This is the shoulder on which the leg will rest.
- It is important that the drilled holes face outward from the seat's center.
- Change the drill bit and drill three ¾" Forstner bit holes 1⅛" deep to fit the legs. *(Photo 9)*
- Hand sand or use a belt or ROS sander to smooth the back of the seat, removing all pencil marks and sanding the glued dowel flush.

Part Two: Preparing to turn three legs

- Create a full scale leg drawing similar to the one shown *(Drawing 11 and Photo 12)* and paste it to a piece of heavy duty construction paper or thin plywood.
- Transfer the major transition points of the design to the template edge.
- (Optional step) On a band saw or scroll saw, carefully cut out the opposite side of the drawing to conform exactly to the desired shape to be turned.

Part Three: Turning three matching legs

- Rough turn each leg blank between centers, then transfer the dimensional information from the drawing template. Place the tenon end at the tailstock end of the lathe and the ball foot end at the headstock end. *(Photo 13)*

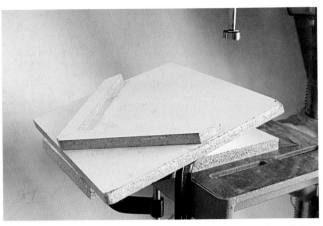

8. A leg hole drilling fixture with a table angle of 15 degrees clamped to the drill press.

9. Drilling the smaller leg hole centered on the larger shoulder, using the alignment line to be sure of squareness.

- Turn the shape to match the drawing, checking frequently to assure the correct shape. *(Photo 14)*
- Turn the leg tenons to exactly ¾" diameter, using a parting tool and your calipers to get a snug fit for the seat hole.
- Sand to final grit.

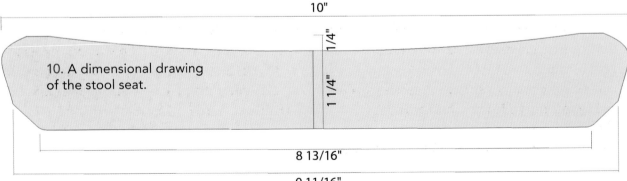

10"

1/4"

1 1/4"

1/4"

10. A dimensional drawing of the stool seat.

8 13/16"

9 11/16"

11. A full scale profile of the leg.

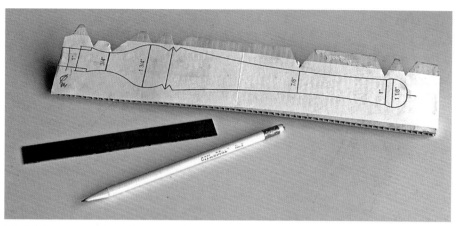

12. Make a template for transferring the template dimensions to the leg blank.

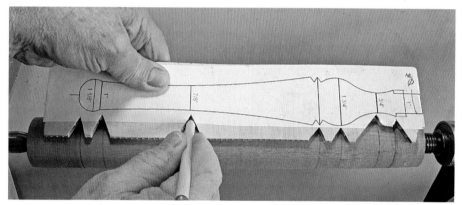

13. Using the template, transfer the major transition points to the blank.

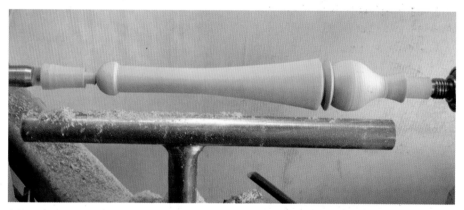

14. A leg turned to the drawing dimensions and ready for sanding.

- Part off the leg at the ball foot end (headstock end), using your skew chisel or shallow fluted gouge.
- On the band saw, shorten the tenon if required to 1" to fit the drilled seat hole with ⅛" glue clearance.
- Repeat this activity for the additional two legs.

Part Four: Completing the stool
- Glue in the legs using yellow woodworker's glue. If the leg fit is tight you may need to "persuade" the fit with a dead blow mallet.
- Finish the seat and legs.

15. A custom carving mallet is a good addition to any workshop.

A Carving Mallet

Objectives
- Complete another simple spindle project, one for you to design and size to fit your hand.

Supplies
- Hardwood stock 3" x 3" x 10" ash, hickory, maple, or similar.

Discussion
Everyone needs a mallet. To get the mallet comfortable in your hand, stop the lathe frequently and grip the handle areas to feel the fit.

Activity
- Rough out the stock and remount it into a four jaw scroll chuck with a solid, square tenon, and add the tailstock for additional support.
- Turn the mallet handle at the tailstock end of the project, checking it frequently to assure it fits your hand in both length and diameter.
- Shape the "working end" at the headstock end of the wood. Allow sufficient distance between the project end and the four jaw scroll chuck for parting off later.
- Remove the tailstock and carefully clean up the end of the handle.
- Reduce the diameter at the headstock end and part off.

16. Spin tops—fun, quick, and good skew chisel practice.

Spin Tops

Objectives
- Create a quick, fun project.
- Practice using the skew chisel to develop personal skill.

Supplies
- Hardwood 2–3" square x 4" long.

Tools & Equipment Required
- Live center and spur drive.
- Four-jaw scroll chuck.
- Spindle roughing gouge.
- Parting tool.
- Skew chisel.
- Color markers for decoration.
- Wax for finish.

Discussion
As the top is turned it can be decorated with color, burn wires, or…? Be sure to part off the point area carefully to get a clean cut that will allow the top to spin smoothly. Keeping the spin point low in the design will allow for more stable and longer spins. Experiment!

17. Use the skew chisel to peel cut the finger top.

Activity
- Set the lathe speed to approximately 1800 RPM and mount the wood between centers and turn it round with the spindle roughing gouge.
- Add a tenon to match your chuck and remount the blank in the four jaw scroll chuck. Re-true the blank if necessary.
- Using the skew chisel (Photo 17), make several "peel cuts" to reduce the diameter of the end

to slightly larger than required to finger spin the top. Keep the long point of the skew chisel toward the headstock end during this cut. Take several small cuts, reducing the shaft diameter in steps.

- Using the long point end of the skew chisel, make planing cuts to smooth out the finger spinning end. *(Photo 18)*
- Still using the skew chisel, make a "V" cut to clean up the upper surface of the top's face. *(Photo 19)* Allow a small clearance angle between the tool and the vertical surface being cut.
- Sand and complete the upper surfaces, adding any decoration or colors to make the top more interesting.
- Starting about ½" to the left of the desired bottom of the top, make a "V" cut with your skew chisel. Enlarge the "V" cut from both the left and right sides, deepening and widening the cut. When the diameter is very small, hold the handle of the top in one hand and continue the "V" cut until the base is parted off. *(Photo 20)*

Remember to keep a small clearance angle between the tool and the wood being cut. Focus on making clean, continuous cuts from both sides.

18. Use a planing cut to smooth the finger top.

19. A "V" cut will clean up the top face.

20. Parting off with a skew creates the spin point at the same time.

21. Baseball bats are simple curves, but very long projects.

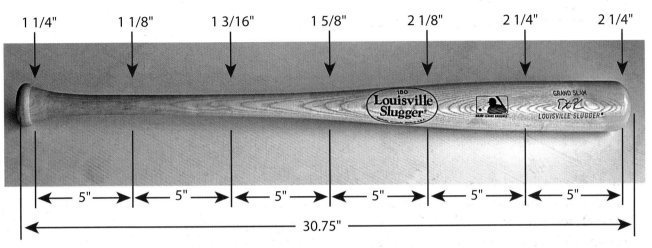

1 1/4"   1 1/8"   1 3/16"   1 5/8"   2 1/8"   2 1/4"   2 1/4"

←— 5" —→ ←— 5" —→ ←— 5" —→ ←— 5" —→ ←— 5" —→ ←— 5" —→

←————————————— 30.75" —————————————→

22. Here is a baseball bat with the dimensions marked every five inches.

Turning a Baseball Bat

Objectives

- Complete another practical project while dealing with a longer and less stable piece of wood.

Supplies

- Maple, ash, or hickory ball bat stock, 2½" x 2½" x 32". The stock must be straight grain and free of knots and defects.

Discussion

Professional baseball bats come in several lengths and weights. The image above is "typical" and you may wish to measure up a different bat for your project. The difficulty in this project is related to the length of the project. The longer stock will tend to "whip" and vibrate in the center due to the wood flexing. Use light cuts with a sharp tool and keep the lathe speed high.

Activity

- Mount the blank on the lathe with a spur drive and live center and turn the blank round.
- With a ruler, transfer the measurement lines to the rough out blank.
- With a parting tool and calipers, transfer dimensions at the marked locations.
- With spindle roughing gouge or shallow fluted gouge, turn the bat to its final dimensions, starting at the tailstock end.
- Sand and finish on the lathe.
- With a parting tool, reduce the end dimensions and cut the project free with a hand saw.
- Sand and finish the ends.

Appendix II
Lathe Maintenance

Supplies
- Disposable gloves.
- Fine grit (220) sandpaper, 0000 steel wool to remove rust and debris.
- Plastic Morris Taper cleaner to clean out both headstock and tailstock tapers.
- Mill bastard file to remove nicks and scratches from the tool rest and tailstock quill.
- Wrenches to fit all nuts & Allen screws on your lathe.
- Old toothbrush to dislodge debris from components.
- Spur drive/live centers to check headstock/tailstock alignment.
- WD 40™/paste wax/silicon spray to allow components to move freely.
- Paper towels and rags for routine cleanup.
- (A double-ended Morris taper alignment fixture may be needed if your lathe has a rotating headstock.)

Discussion
Lathe maintenance is an ongoing set of tasks that must be routinely performed to get the best out of any lathe. The amount and type of maintenance a lathe requires is related to frequency of use, shop environment, the kind of turning done, the age of the lathe and even its mechanical construction. With just a few minutes' time, most of the caretaking can be easily accomplished and the result will be increased enjoyment of your time at the lathe.

Daily maintenance
- **Clean the tapers.** Cleaning the inside of the Morris Tapers will keep debris from accumulating. If sawdust or other debris builds inside a taper the drives may slip. Even more seriously, the drives may lock in the taper, making it difficult or sometimes impossible to remove. Green plastic taper cleaners *(Photo 1)* are readily available from all turning suppliers and should be an essential accessory for every wood turner.
- **Clean the ways and the tool rest and apply lubricant.** *(Photo 2)* Most debris accumulates on the tool rest and the ways. This accumulation will make the tool rest difficult to move and adjust. Daily cleaning means rubbing these areas with steel wool and applying silicon spray. Do not wax the ways as more debris will attach itself to the wax and just make the problem worse.

1. Use a green taper cleaner every day.

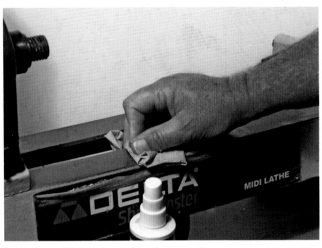

2. Clean the ways and only use silicon spray to lubricate.

3. The headstock threads should be cleaned with a soft brush.

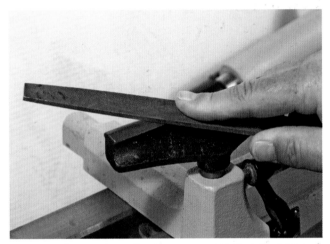

4. Filing the tool rest removes accumulated nicks and gouges.

- **Clean head stock threads.** *(Photo 3)* Sawdust will also accumulate on the threads to the headstock and limit the ability to properly seat a chuck. An old toothbrush or small brass brush will make quick work of this cleaning operation.

Weekly maintenance

- **File tool rest nicks.** *(Photo 4)* A small inexpensive file will quickly remove the nicks and abrasions from the soft iron tool rest. These nicks prevent the tool from moving smoothly through the cut. Check the rest and file away any nicks. You may need to follow the filing with 220-grit sandpaper to further smooth out the abrasions. Follow this with wax or silicon spray.

- **Clean the bottom of the tailstock assembly and the tool rest banjo.** *(Photo 5)* While we clean the top we also need to check and clean the bottom of the mating components to allow them to continue to slide smoothly. Additionally, the locking nut of their cams can slip a little and not allow positive locking. A crescent wrench can easily tighten the nut a fraction of a turn and fix this issue.

- **Remove abrasions from the tailstock quill.** *(Photo 6)* If the quill's locking lever is not tightened correctly into the matching slot, it will damage the quill itself by creating "mushrooms" of soft metal that inhibit the

A Lesson Plan for Woodturning | 91

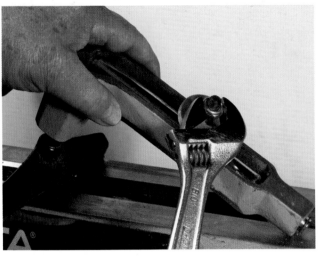

5. Adjusting the banjo may be needed periodically.

6. Filing the quill is necessary when it has been abused by improper locking.

7. Cleaning out the motor's cooling vent will allow it to last much longer.

quill's free movement. To correct this, remove the quill by backing out the locking lever and cranking the quill handle to its full clockwise extension. Examine the quill for abrasions and file them away. Add silicon spray before reassembling the tailstock.

- **Keep the motor running cool.** *(Photo 7)* Smaller lathes have their motors mounted directly below or behind the dustiest lathe areas. Occasionally use pressurized air to blow out any accumulated debris that may obstruct the cooling fan's air circulation.

Occasional maintenance

- **Check and dress drive belts.** Drive belts wear and break before we know it. If they are cross-mounted they will wear more rapidly. Check them occasionally and be sure to have a replacement belt available when you need it.
- **Prevent electrical shorts.** Power cords can rub and abrade, causing electrical shorts or even a fire. Check where all electrical cords are run and eliminate all possible areas of rubbing. Electrical plugs themselves can accumulate dust and should be closed with a childproof plug protector when not in use.
- **Lubricate mechanical variable speed drives.** Many older lathe models and mid-size variable speed lathes use a mechanical mechanism that adjusts the pulley diameter to change

lathe speeds. The collection of springs, pulleys and sliding mechanical components requires checking, cleaning, and lubrication to allow them to run smoothly.

- **Headstock/Tailstock alignment.** On lathes that have a headstock that can be rotated outward and returned to its inline location, this realignment should be regularly checked. The position of the aligning detent should cause the headstock to realign perfectly with the tailstock. Check this alignment by placing a live center in the tailstock and a spur drive in the headstock, bring them close together and lock then in place. The points should be in exact alignment. If not, the lathe's headstock rotation must be corrected.

Appendix III
Additional References

A-B-C-D
- **Anchor** the tool to your body, the tool rest, and the wood surface.
- Rub the **bevel** against the wood.
- Raise the handle toward the flute to **cut** the wood.
- Always cutting **downhill** to the grain whenever possible.

Banjo
The mechanical device that holds the tool rest and allows it to move along the ways of the lathe.

Between centers
A term used to describe wood held with a drive center in the headstock and a revolving live center in the tailstock.

Bevel
The portion of the tool immediately behind the cutting edge which supports the tool against the wood surface.

Center line
The imaginary line connecting the headstock to the tailstock passing directly through the spur drive point and the live center point.

Flute of the tool
The open groove cut in the top of the gouge to create a path for the cut chips to be expelled.

Live center
The revolving mechanism that supports the turning wood at the tailstock end of the lathe; generally a ball bearing drive with a small point in the center.

Morris taper
The tapered shape of the holes in the headstock and tailstock into which are fitted matching taper centers. MT #1, MT #2, and MT #3 are the designations of the specific taper sizes used in woodturning lathes. The most common is MT #2.

Open/close the tool
Opening up a tool is the process of exposing more of the cutting edge to the wood surface and increasing the amount of wood surface engaged. Closing is the opposite.

Parting off
The act of separating the project from the remaining wood still held on the lathe. This is usually accomplished with a parting tool or skew chisel.

Quill
The piston located in the tailstock and operated by an external crank. Its purpose is to advance its contained live center for securing wood between centers or for drilling depth holes.

Rubbing the bevel
Allowing the bevel of the cutting tool to rest against the wood before and during the cutting process.

Sharpening
The process of restoring the cutting edge of a lathe tool. A light redressing of the cutting edge as opposed to grinding away metal.

Spur drive
A barbed device placed in the headstock taper to rotate the wood between centers.

Tear out
The results of fibers being pull from the wood surface due to excessive cutting speed, poor tool sharpness, slow lathe speed, or natural characteristics of the wood species being cut.

Uphill/downhill
The direction relative to the grain. Downhill is toward the more supported fibers during the cut and uphill is toward the least supported fibers during the cut.

Ways
The bed of the lathe connecting the headstock and the tailstock. They contain a channel in which the tool rest/ banjo combination and tailstock assemblies ride.

Project Materials List

Below is a list of supply items required for each exercise. Additional practice stock may be desired for beginning turners to work on developing skill with certain cuts or tools.

	Wood	Tools	Accessories	Disposables
Practicing the Cuts	• 2" x 2" x 10" poplar or similar inexpensive hardwood	• Spindle Roughing gouge • Skew chisel • Parting tool • Shallow fluted gouge	• Spur drive and live center	• None
Tool Handle	• 2" x 2" x 7" hardwood • Inexpensive screw driver	• SRG • Shallow fluted gouge • Parting tool • Skew chisel	• Four jaw scroll chuck • Jacob's chuck and drills	• Sandpaper
Bottle Stoppers	• 2½" x 2½" x 3" blank hardwood • ⅜" hardwood dowel 2¼" inches long	• SRG • Shallow fluted gouge • Parting tool • Skew chisel	• ⅜" drill bit • ⅜" collet chuck with draw bar or Jacob's chuck • Live center	• Wood glue • Sandpaper • Finish • Drilled corks
Napkin Ring Set	• 3" x 3" x 8" hardwood	• SRG • Shallow fluted gouge • Parting tool	• Calipers • MT #2 Jacob's chuck with 1½" Forstner bit • Four jaw scroll chuck • Spur drive and live center	• Sandpaper • Finish
Bud Vase	• 3" x 3" x 3" x 8" hardwood blank	• SRG • Shallow fluted gouge • Parting tool	• Four jaw scroll chuck • Drill bits ¾" or 1" • Calipers • Morris taper Jacob's chuck • Live center • Spur drive	• Sandpaper • Finish
First Dry Bowl	• Bowl blank to fit lathe diameter, 3" thick • 3" x 3" x 4" soft wood for jam chuck	• Deep fluted gouge • Bowl scraper • Parting tool	• Four jaw scroll chuck with worm screw • Drill bit to match the wood screw • Live center • Wall thickness calipers • Face shield	• Sandpaper • Finish
Turning A Platter	• ¾" x 9" x 9" hardwood board	• Deep fluted gouge • Bowl scraper • Parting tool	• Four jaw scroll chuck • Faceplate with glue block attached • Live center • Vernier calipers • Wall thickness calipers • Face shield	• Yellow glue • Sandpaper • Finish • Small plug to cover the live center point
Green Bowls	• Half log with corners trimmed to fit lathe 4–5" deep	• Deep fluted gouge • Parting tool • Internal bowl scraper	• Spur drive • Live center • Four jaw scroll chuck • Wall thickness calipers	• Green wood sealer • Brushes • Kraft paper bag

	Wood	Tools	Accessories	Disposables
Natural Edge Green Bowl	• Half logs trimmed to fit your lathe	• Deep fluted gouge • Parting tool • Bowl scraper	• Four jaw scroll chuck • Jam chuck • Live center • Wall thickness calipers	• Sandpaper • Finish
Goblet	• Hardwood, 3" x 3" x 8"	• SRG • Shallow fluted gouge • Parting tool • Small round nosed scraper	• Four jaw scroll chuck • Tennis ball	• Sandpaper • Finish
Boxes	• Straight grain hardwood 3" x 3" x 8"	• SRG • Shallow fluted gouge • Parting tool • Small round nosed scraper	• Four jaw scroll chuck • Calipers	• Sandpaper • Finish
Optional Project: Candlestick	• Hardwood blank 3" x 3" x 9", one for each candlestick	• SRG • Parting tool • Shallow fluted gouge	• Four jaw scroll chuck • Spur drive • Live center • Calipers & ruler • Candle bit • MT# 2 Jacob's chuck	• Sandpaper • Finish
Optional Project: Small Stool	• 10" x 10" x 2" hardwood for seat • 3 each 2" x 2" x 13" hardwood blanks for legs • ⅜" dowel 1" long	• Deep fluted gouge • SRG • Parting tool • Shallow fluted gouge	• Four jaw scroll chuck with worm screw • ⅜" drill • Spur drive • Live center • Set of full size drawings for legs • Compass • 1⅛" Forstner bit • ¾" Forstner bit • Fixture at 15-degrees to drill leg holes	• Sandpaper • Finish
Optional Project: Spin Top	• Hardwood blank 2"–3" square x 4" long	• Spindle roughing gouge • Skew chisel	• Spur drive & live center • Four jaw scroll chuck	• Sandpaper • Finish • Color markers
Optional Project: Carving Mallet	• Straight grain hardwood 3" x 3" x 9" inches	• SRG • Shallow fluted gouge • Parting tool	• Four jaw scroll chuck	• Sandpaper • Finish
Optional Project: Ball Bat	• Square bat blank 2½" square x 32" long, ash, hickory or maple	• Spindle roughing gouge • Shallow fluted gouge • Parting tool	• Spur drive & live center • Calipers	• Sandpaper • Finish

The collet chuck assembly used in turning bottle stoppers requires:
- A ⅜" collet with a MT #2 taper available from The Little Machine Shop, P/N# 1749, www.thelittlemachineshop.com
- A length of ⅜"-16 all thread cut to length to fit your lathe's headstock available from most local hardware stores.
- A ⅜"-16 knob to fit on the outside of the headstock's hand wheel to secure the assembly with the stopper blank. Also available at the local hardware store or your local woodworking dealer.

Comprehensive Safety Guidelines

Personal safety

1. The use of cell phones and iPods (and the like) is strictly forbidden in the shop.
2. Long, loose hair can easily be caught in revolving machinery and ripped out, causing serious scalp lacerations. Your hair must be tied back or tightly covered when working with machines.
3. Avoid long sleeves, loose clothing, neckties, long hair, necklaces and bracelets or anything that can be caught in moving machinery.
4. No open-toed shoes, floppies or sandals are permitted in the machine areas.
5. Wearing gloves is forbidden while working with machines within the wood shop. Gloves hinder your dexterity and may get caught in moving machinery.
6. If you feel ill, or are on any medication or any other substance that may affect your ability to operate machinery, stop working and seek assistance.
7. Many state laws require that whenever anyone is working in the shop, safety glasses must be worn by everyone. If you have prescription eyeglasses, wear them; eyestrain is a frequent cause of accidents. Safety glasses that fit over your prescription glasses are available (OSHA approved Z87).
8. Always sweep scraps from your workbench or table with a brush or piece of wood rather than with your hands, as there may be sharp or jagged particles among the scraps.
9. You should not use compressed air to clean up the lathe or shop as it creates additional dust and debris.
10. When using air under pressure, be sure the air stream is never directed toward you or any other person.

Workplace safety

1. Any form of horseplay is very dangerous and is strictly forbidden.
2. Do not attempt to distract any person who is using a machine. Do not let yourself be distracted when operating a machine. Wait until you are finished with the operation and shut down the machine before responding.
3. Do not hang anything on fire extinguishers. The area around them should be kept clear so that they may be reached without delay if fire breaks out.
4. Caution anyone you see violating a safety rule. You may save yourself or someone else from serious injury.
5. Remove all scrap and waste wood immediately from the floor where it may be a hazard to you or others. Put all waste wood in a scrap barrel.
6. If you see oil, grease, or any other liquid on the floor, wipe it up immediately to prevent slipping.

Work process safety

1. *Know Your Equipment and Yourself.* Never operate a lathe or use a cutting tool, chuck or other accessory without first understanding its operation and limitations.
2. Never perform a procedure or technique that you are unclear about or uncomfortable with. If you are in doubt, stop and ask for instruction. Know your personal limitations.
3. Plan your work, and work area for safety. Have tools and projects laid out safely and not on top of other machinery.
4. Sharp tools are safest; dull tools are dangerous because they are hard to control and require excess pressure by the operator.
5. Sharp or pointed tools when not in use must be placed in the designated holders, never left lying on the lathe. Always carry tools with

points down. Always hand a tool to another person handle first.

6. Use only good quality wood that you have checked in advance for defects, cracks, knots, etc.

7. All visitors or observers should observe the operator safety zone rule (one arm's length away from the individual operating the machine). They should never stand in the direct path of potential flying objects.

Machine safety

1. *Secure the Wood.* Ensure that the wood is securely held. Turn between centers whenever possible and especially with unbalanced pieces. Use a slow speed when first roughing out a piece.

2. You must be instructed in the correct and safe use of any machine before work can be done using that machine.

3. Immediately discontinue using any machine that is out of adjustment or that sounds unusual until it is checked or repaired.

4. All adjustments to machines must be done while the machine is at a complete stop.

5. All special set ups must be carefully inspected before power is turned on.

6. All wrenches and other tools must be removed from the machine before power is turned on.

7. Keep rags away from machines that are in operation.

8. If you are in doubt about the use of any tool or machine, or about any shop procedure, read the manual and seek assistance.

Stabilizing Green Wood

If you have ever turned green wood from our "urban forest," you have most certainly encountered issues with movement and cracking as the wood dries.

As wood dries, free water is released, reducing the moisture content. Then as cellular water starts to be released the cells begin to shrink. The wood structure also shrinks, mostly radially around the ring structure, to a lesser extent tangentially across the ring structure; and very little along the length of the grain. Each species behaves differently and to a greater or lesser extent. What we try to do is prevent the uneven shrinking from tearing the wood apart, generally along the rays or other weak areas across the ring structure.

Slowing down the drying allows more time for the wood to move and equalize the internal stresses so the wood won't crack. Here are several different techniques in regular use to address this problem.

Stabilizing the green rough-turned vessel

- **Proper rough turning.** Turning to a uniform wall thickness is very important to equalize the drying. Be sure to address the tenon and foot areas, which many times are left too thick, thus allowing cracking to occur in that area. As a rule, leave a wall thickness about 10% of the vessel's diameter.
- **Proper storage.** Storage is important to reduce stress during the drying process. Pack the roughed out vessel with some of its own chips, then place it in one or two brown Kraft paper bags. Label the bags with species, date turned, and the weight. Store the vessel in a cool location that has good air circulation.

As the vessel dries and begins to lose moisture, you can move it to a warmer location. Typically start out placing the wrapped, sealed vessel on the floor in a corner and later move it onto a shelf, then up the shelves to the higher location. Drying can take from weeks to months. Regularly check the moisture content with a moisture meter or by regular weighing.

- **Sealing end grain.** Seal the end grain of the bowl or vessel to prevent more rapid drying through the open end grain fibers. Rapid end grain drying will introduce stress as the end grain dries and shrinks while side grain areas of the vessel have not moved as much. Wax, paraffin, or paint will work to seal the end grain.
- **Complete turning the vessel and add a topcoat finish.** As an alternative, complete the turning to final dimension as rapidly as possible, sand, and finish. Sanding can be difficult with wet wood as the process loads the sandpaper, raises the surface temperature of the vessel and may lead to small surface fractures. Try wet sanding with water and slower lathe speeds.

Finish with penetrating oil or varnish inside and out, load the vessel until it cannot absorb more finish; wipe away the excess and set it aside in a cool airy location to dry. Repeat these steps until the desired finish effect is achieved. As the sealed vessel dries more slowly the stresses are reduced. You may have to accept one of the wood's characteristics: the vessel will change shape.

Water replacement process

Pentacryl and PEG 100 (polyethylene glycol 100) displace the free water with heavier molecules which remain in the cells, preventing the shrinkage. The wood is soaked in the solution until all the water has been osmotically replaced, sometimes 2-3 months. The weight may actually go up, as these molecules are heavier than the water being replaced. Finishing techniques may also be affected by this technique.

Some experiments have suggested that soaking the green wood in denatured ethanol, followed by careful drying, may also reduce the loss while shortening the total drying time. Deformation is still possible.

Cell rupture processes

Boiling, freezing, and soaking in soap solutions all seem to allow the cells to release the cellular water more easily. While the chemistry and botany of these methods are not fully understood, they all have been used successfully to speed up the drying process. Try different techniques by experiment.

The **soap solutions** are usually made of the cheapest liquid detergent cut $^{50}/_{50}$ with water. Soaking the vessel can be from a few days to a few weeks. The seriates in liquid detergents are very similar to the material forming the fiber walls thus weakening the fibers bonds and opening the structure and allowing water to pass through.

Freezing can also assist as water at 4 degrees C actually expands, and the contained cellular water actually ruptures the cell walls and allows the contained water to be dissipated.

One option is to freeze, thaw, and then re-turn the green vessel after a day or two. Some turners report that cracking is substantially reduced while deformation of the wood still remains.

Another technique allows the vessel to be frozen and left in the freezer until the frozen water has desiccated and the vessel is dry. This works only on small thin-walled vessels as the desiccation process is very slow and on larger vessels many take "forever."

Remember that green woodturning is inexpensive, forgiving to the tools, and with the wood movement exciting. If the project does not work out, all you have lost is your time; urban forest wood is free or at least cheap.

Collette Chuck Assembly

The collet chuck assembly used in turning bottle stoppers requires:

- A ⅜" collet with a MT #2 taper available from The Little Machine Shop, P/N# 1749, www.thelittlemachineshop.com.
- A length of ⅜" NC all thread cut to length to fit your lathe's headstock available from most local hardware stores.
- A ⅜" NC knob to fit on the outside of the headstock's hand wheel to secure the assembly with the stopper blank. Also available at the local hardware store or your local woodworking dealer.

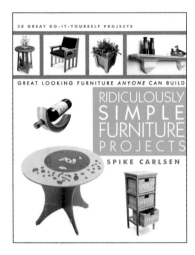
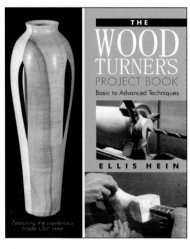
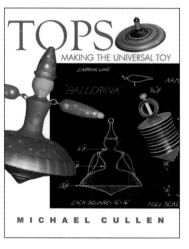
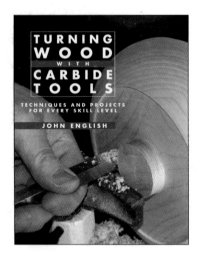
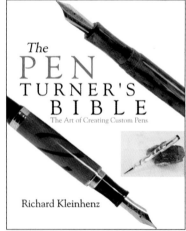
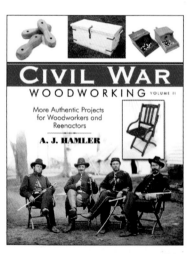